Current
CONTROVERSIES

Cryptocurrencies and Blockchain Technology

Other Books in the Current Controversies Series

Antifa and the Radical Left
The Economics of Clean Energy
Globalization
Historical Revisionism
The Industrial Food Complex
Interference in Elections
Learned Helplessness, Welfare, and the Poverty Cycle
Soft Power and Diplomacy
Tariffs and the Future of Trade
The Two-Party System in the United States
Whistleblowers

Cryptocurrencies and Blockchain Technology

Andrew Karpan, Book Editor

GREENHAVEN
PUBLISHING

Published in 2020 by Greenhaven Publishing, LLC

353 3rd Avenue, Suite 255, New York, NY 10010
Copyright © 2020 by Greenhaven Publishing, LLC

First Edition

Cover image: Wit Olszewski/Shutterstock.com

Library of Congress Cataloging-in-Publication Data

Names: Karpan, Andrew, editor.
Title: Cryptocurrencies and blockchain technology / Andrew Karpan, book
editor.
Description: First edition. | New York : Greenhaven Publishing, 2020. |
Series: Current controversies | Includes bibliographical references and
index. | Audience: Grades 9-12.
Identifiers: LCCN 2019000385| ISBN 9781534505339 (library bound) | ISBN
9781534505346 (pbk.)
Subjects: LCSH: Cryptocurrencies—Juvenile literature. | Blockchains
(Databases—Juvenile literature.
Classification: LCC HG1710 .C785 2020 | DDC 332.4—dc23
LC record available at https://lccn.loc.gov/2019000385

Manufactured in the United States of America

Website: http://greenhavenpublishing.com

Contents

Foreword   **11**

Introduction   **14**

Chapter 1: Are Blockchain-Powered Cryptocurrencies Better than Hard Money?

Overview: What Can You Make and Trade with   **19**
Blockchain?

Umed Saidov

Blockchain is a kind of online public ledger that is secured
cryptographically. Its application as a currency comes from that
security, which proponents suggest can take the place of the
middlemen that our hard money system requires, like banks.

Yes: Cryptocurrencies Are Better than Hard Currency

How Cryptocurrencies Become Real Currencies   **25**

Brandt Redd

A currency is defined by three things: scarcity, verifiability, and
availability, none of which are exclusive to a fiat currency system,
meaning backed by a government. In fact, in a number of ways, a
blockchain-based system can express those qualities better.

Blockchain Offers More than a Currency   **30**

*Michael Crosby, Nachiappan, Pradhan Pattanayak,
Sanjeev Verma, and Vignesh Kalyanaraman*

Bitcoin is more than a currency; its application of blockchain is a
real way to change how money is controlled. A number of potential
applications like Smart Property and Smart Contracts suggest
that blockchain can create new ways to secure the use of money,
automatically performing the function of financial middlemen.

Corruption Is More Difficult with Cryptocurrencies   **34**

Enrique Aldaz-Carroll and Eduardo Aldaz-Carroll

The key to preventing corruption is transparency and accountability,
and cryptocurrencies—with their ledger of transactions—would
make finances more transparent than ever. If governments and
institutions adopted non-anonymous cryptocurrencies, corruption
could be curbed considerably.

No: Cryptocurrencies Are Not Better than Hard Currency

Who Watches the Blockchain?   37

Dirk Baur and Niels Van Quaquebeke

A currency on the blockchain doesn't take the place of
intermediaries, but merely replaces them with a system of
characteristic and system-based trust. A more complex system is not
necessarily a more secure one.

Bitcoin Is an Investment, Not a Currency   41

James Surowiecki

Bitcoin works best as it currently operates: as an investment
appendage inside the current economy. As a currency, it would be
disastrous. Governments would be powerless to affect economic
change and the financial marketplace would be at the mercy of
complex formulas.

The Blockchain Can Hold Money, but It Can Also   47
Be Hacked

Scott A. Wolla

Currencies traded on the blockchain may share a number of
characteristics with hard currencies but, unlike the currencies
of most major nations, there is no way to protect their value and
stability from outside forces.

Chapter 2: Is Blockchain Too Risky to Operate on a Mass Scale?

Overview: A History of Bitcoin on the Blockchain   55

Axel Simon

The first generation of blockchain-powered bitcoin trading involved a
variety of different currencies being traded by relatively small groups
of ambitious investors who publically used the platform's open-
source technology. The second generation of currencies has changed
to emphasize more currency-like characteristics, such as stability,
accessibility, and security.

Yes: Blockchain Is Too Risky

An All-Digital Currency Still Needs a Bank   **60**

Aleksander Berentsen and Fabian Schär

A stable currency system requires a central bank to maintain its day-to-day stability, and no central bank would issue bitcoin on the blockchain. The risk of sanctioning illegal use would be too high.

Blockchain Is As Good As Gold, and That's a Problem   **72**

Bruno Skvorc

The terminology used to describe some of the currencies traded on a blockchain is meant to evoke the trade of valuable minerals like gold. But the fixity of gold is exactly why the industrial world replaced it with fiat currencies that can be inflated and deflated by a central bank.

The Future of Cryptocurrencies Is Uncertain   **77**

Richard Partington

Where will cryptocurrencies go from here? Currently, bitcoin and other cryptocurrencies are still fairly niche, but because of bitcoin's meteoric rise in value in late 2017 and early 2018, many investors are considering giving it a shot. Nonetheless, cryptocurrencies are seldom used in real-world settings, and it is likely that the value of bitcoin has been artificially inflated, creating a bubble and making its future worth difficult to determine.

No: Blockchain Is Not That Risky

Banks Will Come Around   **81**

Michael J. Casey

The adoption of blockchain-based currencies is not something that will happen overnight. Instead, while the banks of some of the world's largest countries may be wary of adopting a currency they can't directly control, it could be some of the world's non-Western countries—seeking a new and inflation-proof solution to managing money—that will be the early adopters who could lead the way.

China on the Blockchain   **85**

Patrick Coate

One non-Western country that has taken to investment on the blockchain is China: by 2016, over 90 percent of bitcoin trade was for the Chinese yuan. This presents a unique case study of the currency's effectiveness and proves that some of its primary obstacles for widespread use are the keepers of the currencies it could replace.

Chapter 3: Is It Possible to Regulate Cryptocurrencies?

Overview: The Blockchain Expands   **92**

University of Cambridge Research

By 2017, research shows that at least three million people actively used cryptocurrencies of some kind. This suggests that they have become a major monetary force, which means new questions have to be asked about how blockchain is used.

Yes: Cryptocurrencies Can Be Regulated and Can Help Regulate the World

Blockchain Can End Money Laundering   **95**

Roy Keidar and Netanella Treistman

Cryptocurrencies like bitcoin have gained a somewhat misguided reputation as a favorite of hackers and money launderers alike, but the tracing mechanisms inherent to the currency's ledger function also mean that these transactions must be made public. A number of regulatory monitoring mechanisms could potentially prevent the ability to trade illegally.

Wikipedia Is a Model for How Blockchain Can Work   **99**

Dirk Baur, Daniel Cahill, and Zhangxin (Frank) Liu

One of the most used and trusted resources on the internet also operates through an open-source ledger: the online encyclopedia Wikipedia. Anyone can edit Wikipedia, but because every edit is public, everyone in the system is able to be part of regulating its accuracy.

The History of Blockchain Regulation   **102**

Andrew Norry

The decentralized nature of cryptocurrencies like bitcoin makes it very difficult to enforce restrictions. Nonetheless, the history of the currency is full of attempts to regulate it, and some of them, like those made in the European Union, have been successful.

No: Cryptocurrencies Are Beyond the Powers of Regulation

Bitcoin Is Not Designed for Regulation   **109**

David Trilling

Cryptocurrencies implicitly undermine government authority, enabling everything from money laundering by organized criminals to the evasion of sanctions by totalitarian countries like North Korea. Because it is exactly those qualities that have made cryptocurrencies appealing to their early adopters, the inability to regulate cryptocurrencies is unlikely to end soon.

The Failure of Bitcoin Regulation   **115**

Andrea Castillo

An attempt to impose regulations on bitcoin transactions in New York state in 2017 resulted in bitcoin-based businesses fleeing the state in droves, which suggests that the cryptocurrency marketplace is implicitly averse to regulation of any kind.

Decentralization Prevents Regulation by a Central   **120**
Authority

Alex Hern

Cryptocurrencies are decentralized by nature, lacking a central authority like a bank to run its database. This makes regulation difficult, and potentially impossible. Furthermore, if one is content with a central banking authority—as Hern claims is the case for most people who are not conducting criminal enterprises—there is no real incentive to use cryptocurrencies.

Chapter 4: Are Blockchain Technologies Too Complex?

Overview: Everything on the Blockchain   **127**

Stefaan Verhulst

The innovation of blockchain offers a secure way to move information, whether it is a currency or even votes in an election. Proponents of these new solutions hold that they can dramatically change everyday life and reduce the need for the kinds of safety apparatuses built into transactions in a global world.

Yes: Blockchain Is Too Complex for Everyday Use

Blockchain Is a Complex Solution Without a Problem   **133**

Greta Bull

Everyday, millions of people around the world are able to use our current financial system, and without even thinking about it are able to enjoy the consumer protections that it offers. A new currency system would require all of them to be renegotiated in pursuit of benefits that the majority of users would not be able to enjoy.

A Critical Case Study of Blockchain in the   **138**
Developing World

Thalia Holmes

Advocates often consider the use of blockchain in a number of
developing nations in Africa as a sign of its possible application.
A more critical examination shows that most of the benefits are
incremental and low-key and do not relate in any specific way to
blockchain itself.

Bitcoin Mining Is an Environmental Hazard   **148**

Christopher Malmo

Bitcoin is among the most widely-accepted cryptocurrencies being
traded today, but the computing energy required to process and
"mine" bitcoin has already caused massive amounts of environmental
damage, with one facility in Mongolia responsible for emitting as
much CO_2 in a single hour as a car driving 203,000 kilometers.

No: Blockchain Is Simple Enough

The Blockchain Is Just a Ledger   **152**

Michael J. Casey and Paul Vigna

Fundamentally, there is not much difference between the blockchain
and double-entry bookkeeping, a practice that dates back to the late
1400s. What appeared radical then is commonplace now, and the
same will apply to blockchain.

Voting on the Blockchain   **161**

Benjamin Freed

Experiments using blockchain to securely vote during a number of
2018 elections show that the technology, on the user level, can be
designed for use by average citizens and consumers alike.

Organizations to Contact   **166**
Bibliography   **171**
Index   **174**

Foreword

"Controversy" is a word that has an undeniably unpleasant connotation. It carries a definite negative charge. Controversy can spoil family gatherings, spread a chill around classroom and campus discussion, inflame public discourse, open raw civic wounds, and lead to the ouster of public officials. We often feel that controversy is almost akin to bad manners, a rude and shocking eruption of that which must not be spoken or thought of in polite, tightly guarded society. To avoid controversy, to quell controversy, is often seen as a public good, a victory for etiquette, perhaps even a moral or ethical imperative.

Yet the studious, deliberate avoidance of controversy is also a whitewashing, a denial, a death threat to democracy. It is a false sterilizing and sanitizing and superficial ordering of the messy, ragged, chaotic, at times ugly processes by which a healthy democracy identifies and confronts challenges, engages in passionate debate about appropriate approaches and solutions, and arrives at something like a consensus and a broadly accepted and supported way forward. Controversy is the megaphone, the speaker's corner, the public square through which the citizenry finds and uses its voice. Controversy is the life's blood of our democracy and absolutely essential to the vibrant health of our society.

Our present age is certainly no stranger to controversy. We are consumed by fierce debates about technology, privacy, political correctness, poverty, violence, crime and policing, guns, immigration, civil and human rights, terrorism, militarism, environmental protection, and gender and racial equality. Loudly competing voices are raised every day, shouting opposing opinions, putting forth competing agendas, and summoning starkly different visions of a utopian or dystopian future. Often these voices attempt to shout the others down; there is precious little listening and considering among the cacophonous din. Yet listening and considering, too, are essential to the health of a democracy. If controversy is democracy's lusty lifeblood, respectful listening and careful thought are its higher faculties, its brain, its conscience.

Current Controversies does not shy away from or attempt to hush the loudly competing voices. It seeks to provide readers with as wide and representative as possible a range of articulate voices on any given controversy of the day, separates each one out to allow it to be heard clearly and fairly, and encourages careful listening to each of these well-crafted, thoughtfully expressed opinions, supplied by some of today's leading academics, thinkers, analysts, politicians, policy makers, economists, activists, change agents, and advocates. Only after listening to a wide range of opinions on an issue, evaluating the strengths and weaknesses of each argument, assessing how well the facts and available evidence mesh with the stated opinions and conclusions, and thoughtfully and critically examining one's own beliefs and conscience can the reader begin to arrive at his or her own conclusions and articulate his or her own stance on the spotlighted controversy.

This process is facilitated and supported in each Current Controversies volume by an introduction and chapter overviews that provide readers with the essential context they need to begin engaging with the spotlighted controversies, with the debates surrounding them, and with their own perhaps shifting or nascent opinions on them. Chapters are organized around several key questions that are answered with diverse opinions representing all points on the political spectrum. In its content, organization, and methodology, readers are encouraged to determine the authors' point of view and purpose, interrogate and analyze the various arguments and their rhetoric and structure, evaluate the arguments' strengths and weaknesses, test their claims against available facts and evidence, judge the validity of the reasoning, and bring into clearer, sharper focus the reader's own beliefs and conclusions and how they may differ from or align with those in the collection or those of classmates.

Research has shown that reading comprehension skills improve dramatically when students are provided with compelling, intriguing, and relevant "discussable" texts. The subject matter of these collections could not be more compelling, intriguing, or urgently relevant to today's students and the world they are poised to inherit. The anthologized articles also provide the basis for stimulating, lively, and passionate classroom debates. Students who are compelled to anticipate objections to their own argument and identify the flaws in those of an opponent read more carefully, think more critically, and steep themselves in relevant context, facts, and information more thoroughly. In short, using discussable text of the kind provided by every single volume in the Current Controversies series encourages close reading, facilitates reading comprehension, fosters research, strengthens critical thinking, and greatly enlivens and energizes classroom discussion and participation. The entire learning process is deepened, extended, and strengthened.

If we are to foster a knowledgeable, responsible, active, and engaged citizenry, we must provide readers with the intellectual, interpretive, and critical-thinking tools and experience necessary to make sense of the world around them and of the all-important debates and arguments that inform it. We must encourage them not to run away from or attempt to quell controversy but to embrace it in a responsible, conscientious, and thoughtful way, to sharpen and strengthen their own informed opinions by listening to and critically analyzing those of others. This series encourages respectful engagement with and analysis of current controversies and competing opinions and fosters a resulting increase in the strength and rigor of one's own opinions and stances. As such, it helps readers assume their rightful place in the public square and provides them with the skills necessary to uphold their awesome responsibility—guaranteeing the continued and future health of a vital, vibrant, and free democracy.

Introduction

When you owe somebody money, you may write an "I owe you" note to help you and your lender remember. If you actually get around to paying the debt off, the note you've written down is as good as the money you're going to pay. In one way or another, this is how modern currency works; we're always transferring debts, from governments to banks and from banks back to you. Because blockchain technology—a list of records that is constantly growing and is connected by cryptography— is fundamentally about using digital space to keep information secure, it has been a magnet for cryptocurrency advocates. Cryptocurrencies are digital assets that can be exchanged and are secured by cryptography. Cryptocurrency proponents see it as a way to use money unattached to government-issuing bodies, which they argue is merely a relic of the pre-internet era.

From this perspective, blockchain is simple enough. The amount of information that a line of code can contain is practically limitless, so why should currency be tethered to physical or geographic locations? Because most of the world doesn't use bitcoin, the currency is associated with dark sides of the internet and unseen actors, but on the face of it, bitcoin is an argument for transparency. Cryptocurrency operates on a ledger in which an endless number of transactions can be coded, and it is in those records that relative value can be calculated and agreed upon by users. The logic of early cryptocurrencies like bitcoin takes this model even further and makes the ledger public, with each transaction traceable along a line that connects every transaction together: the money paid for one good or service can then be traced directly to what it was used for after that, with this continuing in an infinite line. Money can never be lost or stolen, bitcoin's advocates argue, as it takes the power to control it from the hands of banks and governments and spreads it to the masses. In this sense, it serves as a metaphor for a way of thinking about the internet and about whether it has the potential to offer a different, more democratic kind of human relations.

But is it any better? The rhetoric of progress tells us to presume that a new invention is an improvement over what replaced it, but a responsible and reflective approach to our greater environment demands we consider the newest technological innovations with the kind of scrutiny that, in the past, was not applied to the steam engine and the nuclear warhead. Because of the fixation on creating something new, technological innovations are particularly susceptible to accidently recreating things that already exist and, in the case of bitcoin, solving a problem that may not actually exist. Before you heard of bitcoin, did you want it?

The question is not a rhetorical one. Central to the conceit of bitcoin are extraordinarily complicated, computer-generated mathematical problems that are, in turn, solved by massive computers run and programmed by engineers who are often called "miners." This process generates the "coins" that are the basis of what is traded. [1] They are comparable to the role that resources like gold or silver have played in the long history of our own currencies. But to what extent does this comparison hold? "It takes more energy to produce $1 worth of bitcoin…than $1 worth of copper or gold," reports Max Krause and Thabet Tolaymat, authors of a study on the subject that was published in the peer-reviewed journal *Nature Sustainability*. [2] In this model, the use of bitcoin seems not unlike the invention of the SUV, considered by some to be an energy-consuming monster of vanity that is softly killing the planet.

At odds with bitcoin's openness and transparent logic is the mystery it shrouds itself in. There is no venerable Chairman of the Federal Reserve to whom we can turn when considering bitcoin. The designers of bitcoin prefer to stay in the dark and are, in fact, unknown by the public. This is a smart decision on their part, considering the use of bitcoin in facilitating illegal transactions, as it is a commonly used currency on the so-called "dark net" of gun and drug trading. But some argue that bitcoin could be used to prevent crimes, asserting that public users of bitcoin would be traceable and there would be no taxpayer dollars disappearing into the hands of faraway contractors, written off as mysterious but necessary embezzlement. Bitcoin, more than anything else, is all about receipts. The transparent future imagined by bitcoin evangelists is one in which these receipts follow us forever, meaning we can never be stolen from without realizing it.

In this way, bitcoin is less about the actual hard facts of its use than about the debate over its potential uses and what it says about its users. The nature of venture capital-funded expenditures is that they will economically flow top-down, but what about the average consumer? What do cryptocurrencies and, in a more general sense, blockchain technology have to offer besides investment opportunities for those bored by simply exchanging stocks?

The answer may be more than just a new way to move millions of dollars. Many have argued that the technology upon which bitcoin's monetary value is stored could have civic applications. "Digital voting can be done on a transparent ledger, in real-time, over the internet, from anywhere in the world, with voting security that is unhackable, with the right blockchain," writes Jonathan Chester in *Forbes*, presenting one such application.[3] In this future, blockchain would provide an avenue to allow everyone in a representative democracy to vote once and to do this from his or her phone, a technological product that would allow for maximum participation and limited fraud. On the other hand, in such a system "undetectable changes . . . could occur in transit," as Marian Schneider warns in his capacity as president of Verified Voting, a respected nonprofit on the subject of democracy, suggesting a fear that even the most secure codes could be hacked by stakeholders eager to change the results of an election.[4] Other possible uses for blockchain technology include creating digital IDs that would allow all your personal information to be more secure than traditional website logins and passwords, as well as new ways to track purchase information for items like weapons in the event that they're used in a crime.

Blockchain is what we make of it, and the arguments in *Current Controversies: Cryptocurrencies and Blockchain Technology* present different theories about how these technologies can be used. Technology means, to some extent, that we are the architects of our own destiny. The new is always mysterious, but through considering these debates, it will hopefully feel less opaque.

Notes

1. "Everything you need to know about the blockchain," Arjun Kharpal, *CNBC*. https://www.cnbc.com/2018/06/18/blockchain-what-is-it-and-how-does-it-work.html

2. "Mining Cryptocurrencies Is More Energy Intensive Than Actual Mining, Researchers Say," Nicole Nguyen, *BuzzFeed News*. https://www.buzzfeednews.com/article/nicolenguyen/mining-cryptocurrencies-energy-mining-metals?bftwnews&utm_term=4ldqpgc#4ldqpgc

3. "How Can We Increase Voter Turnout? Bitcoin May Be The Answer," Jonathan Chester, *Forbes*. https://www.forbes.com/sites/jonathanchester/2018/11/05/how-can-we-increase-voter-turnout-bitcoin-may-be-the-answer/#5574d79e7c7f

4. "West Virginia to introduce mobile phone voting for midterm elections," Donie O'Sullivan, *CNN*. https://money.cnn.com/2018/08/06/technology/mobile-voting-west-virginia-voatz/index.html

CHAPTER 1

Are Blockchain-Powered Cryptocurrencies Better than Hard Money?

What Can You Make and Trade with Blockchain?

Umed Saidov

Umed Saidov holds an MBA from the European Institute of Business Administration and is the founder of Oqulent LLC, an investment research company focused on blockchain technology and crypto assets.

Blockchain technology is the "engine" that powers cryptocurrency networks and it is rapidly gaining recognition among businesses.

But what exactly is it? How does it work? And how does it generate economic value?

What Is Blockchain?

In essence, blockchain is a cryptographically secured ledger that tracks transactions on a decentralized network. Decentralized networks, like those of bitcoin, Ethereum, Cardano, etc., are a collection of computers that are self-managed by a consensus mechanism—a set of rules that dictate how data is recorded, shared, and synchronized throughout the network.

How Does Blockchain Work?

Blockchain's theoretical foundation fuses mathematics, computer science, game theory, and cryptography. There are several key components that together make blockchain tick.

- **Hash Function**: Cryptographic hash functions are central to blockchain technology. They are used to "chain-link" blocks. The hash function has two important features that help it maintain the security of blockchain.

Hash functions are one way, or asymmetric. They compress an input, or message, of any length into an output of a predetermined length, or hash value. The hash value of an input is easy to calculate, but it is impractical to decipher the input from the hash value.

Hash functions are deterministic. For a given input, there is exactly one resulting hash. Changing any single character in that input changes the hash value. The same input always produces the same output.

- **Public Key Cryptography:** Cryptocurrency networks use private and public keys to generate spending transactions and verify their validity. A private key is a value randomly generated by a digital wallet. It serves as a unique password or authorization code. A public key is the equivalent of an account number. It is generated together with the private key and is mathematically linked to it. A public key or its hash value is known to the entire network.

Every time users conduct a transaction, their wallet cryptographically signs for it using their private key. These digital signatures serve like fingerprints, cryptographically connecting the transaction with the holder of the private key. The network verifies each transaction using the combination of public key and the digital signature. If these match, the network approves the transaction, which then gets added to the blockchain. The public key cryptography allows the network to ensure that only the person with the private key can spend the funds associated with a particular digital wallet.

- **Blockchain:** A self-propagating ledger that resides on a network. Every block on the ledger consists of a header and a set of transactions that are validated by the network at predetermined time intervals. Each block has its own hash signature connecting it to a previous block. The network constantly updates and checks the validity of all these blocks. Changing any single character in that block invalidates it.

- **Mining:** Mining is the process of validating blocks on a network that uses proof-of-work (PoW) as its consensus mechanism. Participants on these networks are incentivized to earn cryptocurrency by helping to include transactions through the process of mining. Mining requires time and computing power to solve a difficult mathematical problem through trial and error. The output of mining is easy to verify but imposes steep costs on bad actors who seek to tamper with legitimate transactions.

Blockchain technology uses hash functions to cryptographically link and secure blocks, public key cryptography to authorize and verify transactions, and a consensus mechanism to synchronize its network.

While the first version of blockchain appeared on a permissionless network, this is not a strict requirement for blockchain technology to work. Blockchain-based networks can be run by private consortia and can have limited access/membership. Hyperledger, for example, is an open-source project hosted by Linux Foundation that encourages various industries to adopt blockchain technology. IBM and Microsoft are two other important players in this space with similar enterprise-level offerings.

How Does Blockchain Generate Economic Value?

Blockchain's fundamental value stems from its two critical properties: persistence and decentralization. These allow blockchain to record transactions on a cheap, accurate, auditable, and secure network that is always open. These combined qualities not only can reduce economic friction in value chains, they can also replace some economic intermediaries, as their functions are taken over by these networks.

So what sectors are likely to experience significant blockchain-driven change?

- **Banking:** Despite its fairly nascent stage, blockchain has already rendered the old model of cross-border money transfers obsolete. Blockchain-powered money can cross the globe in seconds while traditional methods can take days or weeks. The slowest blockchain network can take up to an hour to confirm transfers, the fastest take 4 to 5 seconds. For reference, ACH transfers take three business days, while domestic wire transfers require several hours and can cost $15 or more. Compare that to the Litecoin network, which took 2.5 minutes to send the equivalent of $99 million to the other side of the world for just $0.40 in fees.

Blockchain could also disrupt commercial banking. From a consumer perspective, blockchain eliminates the need for traditional banks since users can hold, accumulate, and disperse capital without an intermediary. Blockchain networks are cheaper to use than those set up by Visa or Mastercard. With blockchain banking apps and fiat-backed, low-volatility cryptocurrencies on the horizon, traditional banking may be facing an existential challenge.

My prediction? Sooner or later banks will become nodes on a decentralized network run by the US Federal Reserve.

- **Real Estate:** Blockchain is a perfect technology to keep track of property titles. A national database of property titles could benefit consumers, expedite real estate transactions, shrink transaction costs, and potentially reduce insurance and interest rates.

- **Health Care:** The health care industry employs a hodgepodge of IT systems that barely talk to each other. While care providers and insurance companies work with the same patient data, data portability is a huge issue. Often patients have to re-enter the same information at different health care service locations. This system is highly inefficient and fragmented. Blockchain could streamline this process by giving each user access to their records. As the need arises, patients could share their data on the network. SimplyVitalHealth is one of many start-ups in the space that are offering blockchain-based health care solutions.

- **Government/IT Security:** The growing severity of cyberattacks demonstrates that our data remains exposed to hackers and other criminals. Cyberattacks are expected to cause $6 trillion in damages by 2021. The Equifax data breaches put the identities of most Americans up for sale without their consent. Blockchain empowers individuals and could improve security, transparency and auditability in government.

  More broadly, blockchain could become the backbone of many government functions, including elections, procurement services, car registration, identity management systems, record keeping, and social security.

- **Transportation:** Maersk and IBM recently announced a joint venture that will use blockchain to streamline the shipping process. Morgan Stanley estimates that block chain-related revenue opportunities could reach $500 billion.

Challenges

Regulation is the major hurdle to mass blockchain adoption. Blockchain's properties, including its open architecture, make it difficult to define it within our traditional legal systems. Custody of assets is a big challenge.

There may be legal challenges, but they are not unsolvable even if their solutions may require some innovative thinking. Blockchain pushes the boundaries of capital formation and allocation across the globe. New laws are required to realize its potential without compromising the fundamental principles that govern the current financial system. Once the full economic importance of blockchain is grasped, sensible new regulations will likely follow.

Bitcoin requires considerable energy resources to power its network, consuming 62.24 terra-watt hours — enough to power all of Switzerland. Such steep energy requirements have evoked criticism, but the space is exploring less costly alternative consensus mechanisms. One potential fix may be proof-of-stake (PoS), a less-energy intensive consensus mechanism.

Conclusion

We live in a world with increasing digitization, a world where our personal data is stored on someone else's computer, where ideas can reach millions at the speed of thought, and where fake news can easily undermine or overwhelm reputable outlets. In this world, trust is in short supply but of incalculable value.

Blockchain empowers the individual. Through a permanent, auditable, and tamper-proof ledger, blockchain can provide that trust and that value.

How Cryptocurrencies Become Real Currencies

Brandt Redd

Brandt Redd has an MBA in organizational communication from Brigham Young University and works as a technology strategist for EdMatrix, an organization that seeks to make learning an enjoyable experience.

Today I'm diverging from the education theme to write about cryptocurrency. I am provoked, in part, by this quote from Alan Greenspan:

> "It [Bitcoin] has to have intrinsic value. You have to really stretch your imagination to infer what the intrinsic value of Bitcoin is. I haven't been able to do it. Maybe somebody else can."

Now, Greenspan should know better than to say something like that. As a fiat currency, the dollar doesn't have any more intrinsic value than Bitcoin. And that's why I decided to write about this. Most of the supposed "Bitcoin Primers" out there are more confusing than helpful. They don't explain how money works or how cryptocurrencies like Bitcoin satisfy the requirements to become a currency.

What Makes a Currency?

Currency is a form of money that accepted by a group of people to exchange value. A functional currency must have three important characteristics:

- **Scarcity**—If you have too much of the currency, it's value will plummet toward zero. So, there must be a limited supply.

- **Verifiability**—You must be able to verify that a unit or token of the currency is valid and not a forgery or imitation.
- **Availability**—Despite scarcity, there still must be a stable supply of the currency to match growth in the corresponding economy.

Precious metals like gold and silver were the first common currencies. They meet all of the foregoing criteria. Gold is scarce; there's a limited amount of it available thereby endowing a small amount of gold with considerable value. It's verifiable; gold has certain characteristics, such as density, malleability and color, that make it easy to distinguish from other materials. And gold is available; while it is not common, gold mines still offer a consistent supply of the material.

One of the difficulties with early uses of gold currency was the complexity of exchange. Merchants had to use a balance or scale to determine how much gold was being offered. To facilitate easier exchange, governments, banks, and other trusted organizations would mint coins of consistent size and weight. This would allow someone to verify the value of a coin without resorting to a balance.

Fiat Currency

"Fiat" means, roughly, "because I said so." Fiat currency has value simply because some trusted entity says it does. It need not have any intrinsic value.

The first fiat money was the banknote. When making a large payment it could be inconvenient or dangerous to move large quantities of coins or bullion. Banks solved this problem for their customers by issuing banknotes. A banknote is a paper that a bank or other entity promises to exchange for a certain amount of coin, gold, or other currency. The bank could keep the corresponding gold locked away in a vault and people could carry more convenient paper certificates.

Beginning in 1863, the United States began issuing gold certificates as a form of paper money or banknote. Certificates like these were backed by stockpiles of gold held in places like Fort Knox. European countries did similar things. With the stresses of late 19th century wars and World War I that followed, countries discovered that they could issue more banknotes than their corresponding stockpiles. This led to a lot of instability until countries figured out how to regulate their currencies. But, by the end of the Great Depression, pretty much every economically developed country had fiat currencies controlled by a central bank. While backed by gold or other reserves, the value of these currencies is not directly tied to the value of gold.

Here's how the USFederal Reserve system works: The Federal Reserve Bank creates the money. Money is issued as currency (the familiar US coins and bills) but also simply as bank balances. Indeed, far more money exists as bank records than in actual physical currency. Originally this was done through careful bookkeeping in bank ledgers. Now it's all done on computers. The money is issued in the form of low-interest loans, primarily to banks, which then lend the money to their customers and to other, smaller banks. Other central banking systems like the European Central Bank work in a similar way.

So, how does fiat money meet our requirements for currency?

- **Scarcity:** Only one entity, the central bank, has the authority to create and issue the currency. The central bank limits the issue of money in order to preserve its value.
- **Verifiability:** Coins and paper money are printed or minted using materials and techniques that are difficult for average people to reproduce but are fairly easy for to verify. Money in the form of bank balances is verifiable because each bank or credit union has accounts with higher-level banks ultimately reaching the Federal Reserve. So, when I write a check from my bank to yours, our two banks contact each other and transfer the value sending records up the banking chain until they reach a common parent bank which may be the Fed. Each bank in the chain verifies that the appropriate balances are in place before allowing the transaction to proceed.

- **Availability**: Central banks can create as much money as they think the economy needs. The primary challenge for central banks is manage the money supply - ensuring both scarcity and availability.

Cryptocurrency

Bitcoin is the first, but by no means the only cryptocurrency. The challenge that the pseudonymous creators of Bitcoin tackled was to achieve the three features of currency—scarcity, verifiability, and availability—in the digital realm. They magnified the challenge by prohibiting a central authority like a government or a central bank. Trust, in the case of Bitcoin, is in the system, not in any particular institution.

- **Scarcity**: The "coin" part of most cryptocurrency names is somewhat misleading. Bitcoin doesn't consist of a bunch of digital tokens that are exchanged. If that were the case it would be hard to prevent double-spending of the same token. Instead, cryptocurrencies work more like bank account balances. Bitcoin has is one, big, public ledger that is duplicated thousands of times. All transactions in the ledger must balance—for one account to receive value, another account must be reduced by the same amount. This ledger is called the block chain and it contains a record of every transaction since the creation of the currency.
- **Verifiability:** Cryptocurrences rely on public-key cryptography to ensure that only the owner of a currency balance can initiate its transfer. The bitcoin owner uses their private key to sign the transfer record and then posts it to the network of block chain replicas. Any entity in the network can use that owner's public key to verify that the transaction is valid and that ownership has been transferred.
- **Availability:** Those who host a copy of the block chain have to perform the cryptographic calculations necessary to verify transaction validity and prevent fraud. Those who do this

fastest are periodically rewarded through the creation of new Bitcoin balances. Because of the reward, maintaining the block chain is known as "mining" and a small industry of Bitcoin mining software and devices has developed. All users of cryptocurrency benefit from this because the more miners exist, the more secure the currency becomes due to the duplication of records and validation.

This is a tremendously clever scheme because it simultaneously ensures a consistent supply of currency, decentralizes operation, and secures the network against manipulation by creating thousands of replicas of the block chain.

Potential Impact

The true value of any currency is the willingness of a community of people to use it for daily transactions. The three requirements, Scarcity, Verifiability, and Availability, combine to cause people to trust a particular currency. When that trust is lost you can get bank runs, hyperinflation, or simple destruction of wealth. Meanwhile, the community rushes to find a new currency.

The advent of the internet with myriad handheld devices capable of initiating transactions makes it possible for multiple currencies to coexist. For the first time in history, people may have a choice among currencies to use in daily transactions. Central bankers, and the sovereign countries that endow them with their power, are appropriately worried. An industry that has historically been immune to competition no longer has that protection.

I think this is a good thing. Just like any other competitive market, competition should incentivize good behavior both from established central banks and from upstart cryptocurrencies.

Blockchain Offers More than a Currency

*Michael Crosby, Nachiappan, Pradhan Pattanayak,
Sanjeev Verma, and Vignesh Kalyanaraman*

*Michael Crosby, Nachiappan, Pradhan Pattanayak, Sanjeev Verma,
and Vignesh Kalyanaraman are researchers at the Sutardja Center
for Entrepreneurship & Technology, which is part of the University
of California, Berkeley.*

A blockchain is essentially a distributed database of records or public ledger of all transactions or digital events that have been executed and shared among participating parties. Each transaction in the public ledger is verified by consensus of a majority of the participants in the system. And, once entered, information can never be erased. The blockchain contains a certain and verifiable record of every single transaction ever made. To use a basic analogy, it is easy to steal a cookie from a cookie jar, kept in a secluded place, than stealing the cookie from a cookie jar kept in a market place, being observed by thousands of people.

Bitcoin is the most popular example that is intrinsically tied to blockchain technology. It is also the most controversial one since it helps to enable a multibillion-dollar global market of anonymous transactions without any governmental control. Hence it has to deal with a number of regulatory issues involving national governments and financial institutions.

However, Blockchain technology itself is non-controversial and has worked flawlessly over the years and is being successfully applied to both financial and non-financial world applications. Last year, Marc Andreessen, the doyen of Silicon Valley's capitalists, listed the blockchain distributed consensus model as the most important invention since the Internet itself. Johann Palychata from BNP Paribas wrote in the *Quintessence* magazine that bitcoin's blockchain,

"BlockChain Technology," by Michael Crosby, Nachiappan, Pradhan Pattanayak, Sanjeev Verma, Vignesh Kalyanaraman, Sutardja Center for Entrepreneurship & Technology, October 16, 2015. Reprinted by permission.

the software that allows the digital currency to function, should be considered as an invention like the steam or combustion engine that has the potential to transform the world of finance and beyond.

Current digital economy is based on the reliance on a certain trusted authority. Our all online transactions rely on trusting someone to tell us the truth—it can be an email service provider telling us that our email has been delivered; it can be a certification authority telling us that a certain digital certificate is trustworthy; or it can be a social network such as Facebook telling us that our posts regarding our life events have been shared only with our friends or it can be a bank telling us that our money has been delivered reliably to our dear ones in a remote country. The fact is that we live our life precariously in the digital world by relying on a third entity for the security and privacy of our digital assets. The fact remains that these third party sources can be hacked, manipulated or compromised.

This is where the blockchain technology comes handy. It has the potential to revolutionize the digital world by enabling a distributed consensus where each and every online transaction, past and present, involving digital assets can be verified at any time in the future. It does this without compromising the privacy of the digital assets and parties involved. The distributed consensus and anonymity are two important characteristics of blockchain technology.

The advantages of Blockchain technology outweigh the regulatory issues and technical challenges. One key emerging use case of blockchain technology involves "smart contracts." Smart contracts are basically computer programs that can automatically execute the terms of a contract. When a pre-configured condition in a smart contract among participating entities is met, then the parties involved in a contractual agreement can be automatically made payments as per the contract in a transparent manner.

Smart Property is another related concept which is regarding controlling the ownership of a property or asset via blockchain using Smart Contracts. The property can be physical such as car, house, smartphone etc. or it can be non-physical such as shares of a company. It should be noted here that even Bitcoin is not really a currency—Bitcoin is all about controlling the ownership of money.

[...]

Existing Market

Blockchain technology is finding applications in both financial and non-financial areas that traditionally relied on a third trusted online entity to validate and safeguard online transactions of digital assets. There was another application "Smart Contracts" that was invented in year 1994 by Nick Szabo. It was a great idea to automatically execute contracts between participating parties. However, it did not find usage until the notion of cryptocurrencies or programmable payments came into existence. Now two programs, blockchain and smart contract, can work together to trigger payments when a preprogrammed condition of a contractual agreement is triggered. Smart Contracts are really the killer application of the cryptocurrency world.

Smart contracts are contracts which are automatically enforced by computer protocols. Using blockchain technology it has become much more easier to register, verify and execute Smart Contracts. Open source companies like Ethereum and Codius are enabling Smart Contracts using blockchain technology. Many companies which operate on bitcoin and blockchain technologies are supporting Smart Contracts. Many cases where assets are transferred only on meeting certain conditions which require lawyers to create a contract and banks to provide escrow service can be replaced by Smart Contracts.

Ethereum has created lot of excitement for its programmable platform capabilities. Ethereum allows anyone to create their own cryptocurrency and use that to execute, pay for smart contracts. Ethereum itself has its own cryptocurrency (ether) which is used to pay for the services. Ethereum is already powering a wide range of early applications in areas such as governance, autonomous banks, keyless access, crowdfunding, financial derivatives trading and settlement using smart contracts.

Also, there are a number of blockchains in existence to support a wide range of applications—not just cryptocurrency. Currently there are three approaches in industry to support other applications and also to overcome perceived limitations of Bitcoin blockchain:

- **Alternative Blockchains** is a system of using the blockchain algorithm to achieve distributed consensus on a particular digital asset. They may share miners with a parent network such as Bitcoin's—this is called merged mining. They have been suggested to implement applications such as DNS, SSL certification authority, file storage and voting.
- **Colored Coins** is an open source protocol that describes a class of methods for developers to create digital assets on top of Bitcoin blockchain by using its functionalities beyond digital currency.
- **Sidechains** are alternative blockchains which are backed by Bitcoins via Bitcoin contract—just as dollars and pounds used to be backed by gold. One can possibly have a thousands of sidechains "pegged" to Bitcoin, all with different characteristics and purposes—all of them taking advantage of scarcity and resilience guaranteed by the Bitcoin blockchain. The Bitcoin blockchain can in turn iterate to support additional features for the experimental sidechains— once they have been tried and tested.

Companies such as IBM, Samsung, Overstock, Amazon, UBS, Citi, Ebay, Verizon Wireless to name a few are all exploring alternative and novel uses of the blockchain for their own applications. Nine of the world's biggest banks including Barclays and Goldman Sachs have recently (Sept. 15, 2015) joined forces with the New York based financial technology firm R3 to create a framework for using the blockchain technology in the financial market. This is the first time banks have come to work together to find applications of blockchain technology. Leading banks like JPMorgan, State Street, UBS, Royal Bank Of Scotland, Credit Suisse, BBVA and Commonwealth Bank of Australia have joined this initiative.

Corruption Is More Difficult with Cryptocurrencies

Enrique Aldaz-Carroll and Eduardo Aldaz-Carroll

Enrique Aldaz-Carroll is a senior economist in macroeconomics and fiscal management at the World Bank. Eduardo Aldaz-Carroll is Chief Technology Officer and a roboticist and electronic systems engineer at Betomorrow UK.

Technological advances have made it possible to dramatically increase the accountability and transparency of public financing to reduce corruption. For example, if a government decides to construct a road, it can now track how each dollar is being spent, identify all the users of the funds, and ensure that only those authorized to spend money do so on originally intended expenses within the permitted time. Fraud and corruption investigations that now take on average 15 months could be performed at the touch of a button and at a fraction of the cost. More importantly, this type of financial tracking would be a deterrent for bribes in the public sector, which amount to between $1.5 trillion and $2 trillion annually, roughly 2 percent of global GDP. This in turn would increase development impact. All it would take is adopting a cryptocurrency and using blockchain software.

The adoption of cryptocurrency—a digital currency that employs cryptography to ensure that transactions are secure—as a mode of payment for a project allows the identification of each user of the money, unlike with traditional modes of payment like notes and coins. Though most popular cryptocurrencies, like bitcoin, are anonymous and only use a key to identify a user, it is possible to include personal information, like the ID number, and make the

"Can cryptocurrencies and blockchain help fight corruption?" by Enrique Aldaz-Carroll and Eduardo Aldaz-Carroll, The Brookings Institution, Febuary 1, 2018. Reprinted by permission. Originally published by the Brookings Institution in its Future Development blog, https://www.brookings.edu/blog/future-development/2018/02/01/can-cryptocurrencies-and-blockchain-help-fight-corruption/.

cryptocurrency non-anonymous. The use of cryptocurrency also allows for instantaneous transactions and borderless transfer-of-ownership ("money with wings"), which reduces transaction time and cost, since financial intermediaries are not needed.

A government or development institution could use an existing non-anonymous cryptocurrency or develop its own and give it a name, such as "cleancoin" for example. The value of the cryptocurrency can be determined by the market or preferably be pegged to a physical currency to reduce volatility (bitcoin for instance has shown very high volatility since its inception).

The adoption of blockchain helps track the use of the cryptocurrency. The blockchain is a continuously growing list of transactions (blocks) made using cryptocurrency that are recorded chronologically. The blockchain is managed by a peer-to-peer network (miners) collectively adhering to a protocol for validating new blocks. Once the transaction data in a block is recorded, it cannot be altered retroactively as it would require altering all the subsequent blocks. As the data is stored in many computers, there is little risk of data loss, and since it is encrypted, the confidentiality of data is maintained. Because the blockchain is a public ledger of all cryptocurrency transactions, it is searchable and can be used to track all transactions.

The lack of anonymity and the tight traceability makes corruption more difficult, unlike with traditional money. Two additional features will help fight fraud and corruption effectively. First, the blocks should contain additional data that typically stored so that there is sufficient information for the purposes of fraud and corruption enforcement. For instance, the block can store the nature of the expense and the project and activity linked to the funds. Second, the verification of a block should include checking that the additional data satisfies the smart contract. A smart contract contains logical clauses programmed in the code that triggers processes according to the terms of a contract. These terms could define the conditions to be met to release funds, dates from which they can be made available, and so on. The satisfaction of the contract helps prevent improper expenses.

These four features can be incorporated using Ethereum technology. Ethereum is an open source software platform based on the use of blockchain that allows for the creation of new cryptocurrency types that are not anonymous and permits the inclusion of additional information in the blocks and the use of smart contract features. With the platform set up, the government or development institution could simply allocate cryptocurrency to the activities as budgeted. Those persons or firms assigned to the activities would be allowed to take the cryptocurrency and spend it in goods and services, with verification being performed in the Ethereum platform according to the set protocol and contract. The verification would be performed by insider or external miners who would be rewarded with a share of the cryptocurrency or through transaction fees.

Access to the cryptocurrency would be provided using software wallets (which do not require having a bank account, an advantage in developing countries with low financial access). The final holders of cryptocurrency can choose to convert it into fiat currency at an exchange market—which could be a primary exchange market run by the development institution or government or a secondary exchange market—or to use it as currency, if the market counterpart accepts it, for further transactions outside the activity.

Cryptocurrency and blockchain could help prevent fraud and corruption, reduce the costs of enforcement thanks to easily accessible information and faster crosschecks, and help supervise implementation and monitor efficiency and effectiveness of spending, increasing development impact.

Who Watches the Blockchain?

Dirk Baur and Niels Van Quaquebeke

Dirk Baur is a professor of finance at the University of Western Australia and Niels Van Quaquebeke is a professor of leadership and organizational behavior at Kühne Logistics University in Hamburg, Germany.

A common idea about the blockchain, the technology that powers Bitcoin and other cryptocurrencies, is that it can "create trust," or allow two parties to make a transaction "without relying on trust."

If true, this means we could create a world without a trusted "man in the middle." We could have financial services without a bank verifying transactions and we could transfer ownership (of a house, for instance) without a lawyer. But this idea is wrong.

The blockchain does not create or eliminate trust. It merely converts trust from one form to another. While we previously had to trust financial institutions to verify transactions, with the blockchain we have to trust the technology itself.

It is also not clear that a blockchain-powered currency (such as Bitcoin) can go mainstream without the backing of a trusted authority. In fact there are hardly any examples of money (including gold) that have ever worked without the backing of a central authority or a sovereign.

When you make a traditional money transfer the bank will first verify that you have sufficient cash, and then debit your account and credit the recipient. Think of the blockchain as a decentralised version of this process. Rather than all of this information being held and verified by the bank, it is done on an "open public ledger".

"The blockchain does not eliminate the need for trust," by Dirk Baur and Niels Van Quaquebeke, The Conversation, November 16, 2017. https://theconversation.com/the-blockchain-does-not-eliminate-the-need-for-trust-86481. Licenced under CC BY-ND 4.0 International.

When someone transfers a Bitcoin, it is verified by "miners" (really powerful computers), then encrypted, and a "block" is added to the ledger.

Because all of the verification is done by the system itself, the idea is that users do not need a trusted central authority. Instead, trust is transferred from one central authority (such as a bank) to many decentralised, anonymous participants (the miners).

But here lies the problem—users must trust the technology and the governance of the system.

What Is Trust?

In economic exchanges there are three kinds of trust: institutions-based, characteristic-based, and process-based.

Institutions-based trust comes from the involvement of a central authority. Think of a commercial bank (and a government insuring deposits in that bank), as in the previous example.

Characteristic-based trust is the trust we have in people mostly because they represent some sort of similarity to us, or show admirable features or values that warrant trust. For example, you are more likely to trust someone from the area where you grew up than someone from elsewhere; you might also trust someone with a similar taste in music, or who simply embodies what you value in life.

Process-based trust arises when previous experiences suggest that the inputs by one party will be predictably reciprocated. This trust often evolves into social micro-rules or norms. For example, most people would generally trust that if they do not harm a person, that person will also not harm them. Likewise, one would trust that others will answer when asked a question.

It follows that trust can be destroyed and lost if the central authority fails, the person you trusted fails, or the process you trusted fails.

When it comes to the blockchain specifically, we can see that there are at least two forms of this trust at play. Because of its complexity many people may find it difficult to trust the process.

But some may choose to trust it when like-minded people use it (characteristic-based trust). Indeed, friends of or nerds in the same sphere as Vitalik Buterin, the founder of the Ethereum cryptocurrency, likely became early adopters of the technology.

Yet, a different kind of trust may also be at play. For instance, when the Ethereum-powered decentralised autonomous organisation (DAO) was hacked, users asked Buterin to respond. This shows that people still need a central authority or will appeal to one if the system fails. Likewise, the fake news that Vitalik had died led to US$4 billion dollars being wiped off the market value of Ethereum. With the assumed loss of the central authority, many also lost their trust in the underlying system.

This may not be ideal but a truly open public blockchain (that is, one without any central authority behind it) is unlikely to work.

Analysis of the evolution of money shows that almost all currencies throughout history have had the backing of an authority. This is easy to understand. Think of a raw gold nugget. To be sure about its value you would need to trust a jeweller—a valuation authority. Because this process of identifying the quality of gold takes time, raw gold is not the ideal medium of exchange.

This problem with gold was largely resolved by the creation of the mint. In other words, the minting and standardisation of gold coins reduced the identification costs and thus the need to trust decentralised third parties such as the jeweller. Instead, there was now a need to trust a central authority—the mint.

You also need to trust that the government will accept tax payments in the minted gold coins, and that other people will take the coins as payment for goods and services. More generally, if people lose trust in the authority and the value of a currency, they will try to sell the currency, leading to inflation or even hyperinflation.

All of this shows that gold and any other form of money—including cryptocurrencies—are not "trustless."

The importance of the trusted central authority can also be understood in the case that a currency is destroyed. For example, when the Roman empire fell, the central authority collapsed and so did the currency it backed. Process-based trust collapsed as well, which shows that the process only worked because of the institution.

If history is any guide, privately created money such as Bitcoin or any other blockchain-based currency is unlikely to become globally accepted without a trusted central authority. This means that an "open" blockchain will not succeed. Although a "closed" blockchain, with the backing of a central authority, might work, it would be very different to the core feature of Bitcoin and the blockchain—decentralization.

Bitcoin Is an Investment, Not a Currency

James Surowiecki

James Surowiecki is the author of The Wisdom of Crowds *and a senior story producer at* Vice News Tonight.

E arlier this year, Jack Dorsey, cofounder of Twitter and CEO of Square, declared that Bitcoin would become the world's "single currency" within a decade. What was striking about Dorsey's comment wasn't just the audacious prediction but also the notion that Bitcoin might be useful for something other than speculative investing. After all, even as the financial world has been gripped by cryptocurrency mania over the last year, the "currency" part of cryptocurrencies has receded in importance in the public eye. As a Goldman Sachs executive put it last year, Bitcoin is, at the moment, more of an asset than a currency—it's something people trade, like a stock or bond, rather than something they exchange for goods and services.

That perception reflects reality. The number of Bitcoin transactions (as opposed to trades) has not risen much in the last few years, and one recent academic study suggested that half of those transactions are associated with illicit activity. As a medium of exchange, Bitcoin remains today pretty much what it was in 2010: an interesting complement to the existing monetary system, primarily useful for people interested in avoiding legal authorities or living in societies racked by inflation (like, say, in Venezuela or Zimbabwe).

Still, the dream that cryptocurrency could replace our existing system of fiat money, in which the money supply is controlled by government-run central banks, remains a key part of Bitcoin's appeal. The promise is of a system where the government can't manipulate the money supply, and market competition determines

"Bitcoin would be a calamity, not an economy," by James Surowiecki, MIT Technology Review, April 10, 2018. Reprinted by permission.

which currencies people use. But what would happen if that dream came true? If the dollar and the euro were replaced by Bitcoin, how would the system adapt, and how would the economy and the financial system function?

The simple answer is: not well. Our economies and financial systems are built around fiat money, and they rely on the central bank's control of the currency (and the government's ability to issue debt in that currency) to help manage the business cycle, fight unemployment, and deal with financial crises. An economy in which Bitcoin was the dominant currency would be a more volatile and harsher economy, in which the government would have limited tools to fight recessions and where financial panics, once started, would be hard to stop.

The Opposite of What You Want

To see why this is the case, it's key to recognize the crucial role that the central bank (which in the US is the Federal Reserve) plays to provide what economists call "liquidity" when the system needs it. That's just a fancy way of saying that the central bank can pump money into the system, either by printing it and then lending it to banks (with the idea that they will then inject that money into the system) or by simply buying assets itself. Providing liquidity is especially important in times of financial crisis, because crises lead banks to cut back on lending and savers to pull their money out of banks. In those times, the central bank serves as a lender of last resort, stepping in when otherwise solvent banks are struggling to stay afloat and ensuring that we don't end up with a flood of bank closings.

In an economy run on Bitcoin, these things would be impossible for a central bank to accomplish. A key aspect of the Bitcoin protocol is that the total number of bitcoins is capped at 21 million, after which no more will ever be issued. This makes Bitcoin appealing to many people because something that will never increase in supply is more likely to hold its value. The problem is that in the event of a crisis, there would also be no way to add liquidity to the system, since you can't "print" more bitcoins. The central bank could build up a stash of bitcoins that it could then funnel into the system, but that would do little good because people would know the stash was limited. And in any case, the central bank's demand for Bitcoin would drive up its price, which would make people more likely to hold onto it and less willing to spend it—the opposite of what you want in a financial crisis.

Bitcoin would also make it hard for governments to fight recessions, which they typically do by using what economists call countercyclical monetary and fiscal policy. Central banks slash interest rates, and—as the Federal Reserve did after the 2008 financial crisis—pump money into the system by buying assets (what's known as quantitative easing). And governments try to get the economy moving again by cutting taxes and increasing spending, typically paying for that by borrowing money, as with the Obama-era stimulus package.

Here again, a Bitcoin economy would limit the government's options. Since the central bank would have no control over the currency, it would also have no control over interest rates, and only a limited ability (depending on the size of its Bitcoin stash) to pour money into the economy. Fiscal policy, too, would be close to impotent. Today, when the government runs a deficit, it can have the Fed print money and then borrow that money from the Fed. That adds liquidity to the system. In the Bitcoin world, the government would have to borrow bitcoins to spend. And again, this would make bitcoins more valuable, making people less willing to spend them—the opposite of what you need to fight a recession.

But Don't Worry About It

The good news is that it's an incredibly unlikely future. While the idea of making Bitcoin a universal currency may have impeccable logic to digital-age utopians, in practice it makes little sense. And the design of Bitcoin also makes it difficult to imagine. Since the supply of bitcoins is limited, if the demand for them rises, their value rises, too. But that means that if you own bitcoins, and you think they're going to become more popular, then the sensible thing to do is hold them, since they'll be more valuable tomorrow. That makes people less interested in using bitcoins to actually buy stuff and more interested in treating them as speculative investments— the opposite of what you want in a medium of exchange.

You might think that the same restrictions on supply were true of gold when economies were run on the gold standard. But the supply of gold wasn't fixed. It expanded as people mined more of it. There actually was something of an equilibrium—as economic growth increased the demand for gold, making it more valuable, the rising price encouraged people to mine it, which brought more gold into the system, ultimately keeping the dollar value of gold relatively stable. Between 1800 and 1900, the dollar value of gold gradually rose by small percentages. Bitcoin, by contrast, regularly rises and falls 5 or 10 percent in a single day, purely because of shifts in speculative sentiment. That volatility weakens its usefulness as a store of value (one of the other roles of a currency) and makes it unsuitable for use as a day-to-day medium of exchange, since no one wants to accept a currency if it might be worth 10 percent less a couple of hours from now. In other words, a financial system run on Bitcoin would have all the bad features of the gold standard and few of the redeeming ones.

There are also practical hurdles to making Bitcoin a currency people can use easily. When demand for Bitcoin is high, transaction fees soar as miners raise the price of processing those transactions. At the peak of Bitcoin mania last fall, it could cost as much as $55 a transaction. That was fine when people thought the value of their Bitcoin stash was going to double overnight. But it doesn't work if people want to use Bitcoin to buy pizza or a new TV set. Even more important, Bitcoin cannot scale to deal with the number of transactions a modern economy needs. The system is limited to processing just 420 transactions per minute. Finally, there's the fact that a remarkably small number of people control a remarkably large percentage of all the bitcoins in the world. That gives them the leverage to manipulate prices, and makes it harder for Bitcoin to have the reach it would need to become a real currency.

Choose Your Own Currency!

Of course, bitcoin is far from the only cryptocurrency. Depending on how you count, there are now hundreds, if not thousands, of them. And while they're all built, like Bitcoin, on the blockchain, some have features that might seem to make them more attractive as a potential global currency. Litecoin, for instance, can process more transactions per minute. Monero and Zcash offer genuine anonymity (as opposed to Bitcoin, where every transaction is associated with a given key that can be tracked). And not all cryptocurrencies have a rigid cap on the total number of coins. So perhaps a different cryptocurrency could replace the dollar or euro or yuan—or, more plausibly, we could end up with a system of lots of different private currencies, rather than relying solely on a single medium of exchange.

There's something appealing about the idea of everyone choosing the currency that suits them best, and of cryptocurrencies competing against each other to win the loyalty of consumers and businesses. But in fact the proliferation of cryptocurrencies that we've seen over the past few years makes it less likely, not more, that they will eventually replace fiat money.

The problem with a world in which there are lots of different private currencies is that it massively increases transaction costs. With a single, government-issued currency that's legal tender, you don't have to think about whether or not to accept it in exchange for goods and services. You accept dollars because you know that you will be able to use them to buy whatever you want. Commerce flows more smoothly because everyone has implicitly agreed to use the dollar.

In an economy with lots of competing currencies (particularly cryptocurrencies unbacked by any commodity), it would work very differently. If someone wants to pay you in Litecoin, you have to figure out whether you think Litecoin is a real cryptocurrency or just a scam that could shut down any day now. You have to consider who else might accept Litecoin if you want to spend it, or who would trade you dollars for it (and at what exchange rate and transaction fee). Basically, a proliferation of currencies tosses sand into the gears of commerce, making transactions less efficient and more costly. And any currency that is hard to use is less valuable as a medium of exchange.

Still Great for Money Laundering

This isn't speculative. we actually have a historical example of how this works. In the United States in the decades before the Civil War, there was no national currency. Instead, it was an era of what was called "free banking." Individual banks issued bank notes, theoretically backed by gold, that people used as money. The problem was that the farther away from a bank you got, the less recognizable (and therefore the less trustworthy) a bank's note was to people. And every time you did a deal, you had to vet the note to make sure it was worth what your trading partner said it was worth. So-called wildcat banks sprang up, took people's money, issued a host of notes, and then shut down, making their notes worthless. To be sure, people came up with workarounds—there were volumes that were a kind of Yelp for banking, displaying the panoply of bank notes and rating them for reliability and value. But the broader consequence was that doing business was simply more complicated and slower than it otherwise would have been. The same will be true in a world where some people use Ethereum, others use Litecoin, and others use Ripple.

That doesn't mean that cryptocurrencies are useless. On the contrary, for transactions that one wants to keep hidden from the government (or other authorities), they will remain useful. Buying drugs, laundering money, evading capital controls, protecting your money in countries with hyperinflationary environments: these are all situations where cryptocurrencies can come in handy. But the notion that private cryptocurrencies might soon (or ever) be a meaningful competitor to fiat money for everyday transactions is little more than a pipe dream.

The Blockchain Can Hold Money, but It Can Also Be Hacked

Scott A. Wolla

Scott A. Wolla is a senior economic education specialist with the Federal Reserve Bank of St. Louis.

B itcoin has become a cultural and financial phenomenon. While many people have heard of Bitcoin, far fewer understand it. In short, Bitcoin is a digital currency, or "cryptocurrency," that allows person-to-person transactions independent of the banking system. Bitcoin is not a physical coin that you keep in your purse or wallet. Rather, it is a virtual currency—a digital computer code you store in a virtual wallet in cyberspace and access with a computer or smartphone app. Some see Bitcoin as revolutionary because it allows people to transfer money to each other very easily (like sending an email), even across international borders. Lately, however, many people are buying this virtual currency purely as a financial investment, hoping it will appreciate, rather than using it for transactions. So which is it—currency or financial asset? Or perhaps the line dividing one from the other is not very clear.

Is Bitcoin Money?

Traditionally, currency is produced by a nation's government. In the United States, the US Treasury, through the United States Mint and the Bureau of Engraving and Printing, produces the coins and bills we spend. The Federal Reserve System (the central bank of the United States) distributes money through the banking system. This money is fiat money; that is, its value is not backed by gold or some other commodity. Instead, its value comes from its general acceptance as money. In other words, US dollar bills

"Bitcoin: Money or Financial Investment?" by Scott A. Wolla, Federal Reserve Bank of St. Louis, March 2018. Reprinted by permission.

and coins are useful as money because of the way people use them in the economy.

Money serves three functions in an economy: medium of exchange, store of value, and unit of account. To be an effective medium of exchange, money must be acceptable in exchange for goods and services. Bitcoin can be used as a medium of exchange for a limited number of goods. Bitcoin's credibility as a medium of exchange was enhanced when Richard Branson accepted Bitcoin from the Winklevoss twins for a ride on his spacecraft.[1] While the number of companies that accept payment in Bitcoin has been growing, these transactions still represent a tiny part of the economy. In addition, while Bitcoin was created as a peer-to-peer payment system, many of the Bitcoin transactions that occur between consumers and companies involve "middlemen" who facilitate the transactions by exchanging Bitcoin into conventional currencies.[2] A transaction itself can be costly in both time and money—on average, it takes 78 minutes to confirm a transaction (although it can take much longer) and costs $28 to complete a transaction.[3] In addition, people generally prefer a medium of exchange that maintains stable value over time (as compared with services or a basket of goods). For example, the Federal Reserve's inflation goal is 2 percent annually. If this target is achieved, the US dollar will lose purchasing power at 2 percent per year. The Federal Reserve considers this inflation level to be "price stability"; that is, a rate of inflation that is low and stable enough to be nearly irrelevant to people's economic decisions. Bitcoin's value, however, has not been stable over its history.

Because money also serves as a store of value, the stability of that value is even more important. Bitcoin's value has grown quite dramatically in recent years. Now, volatile prices might not seem to be a threat to the store-of-value function of money when prices are rising; but when prices are falling, people are reminded that *stable value* is an important aspect of *store of value*. For example, Bitcoin has had several periods when prices fell dramatically, including a 20 percent decline in value on the morning of November 29,

2017.[4] In fact, Bitcoin experienced five different episodes of at least 20 percent losses (what market watchers describe as a "bear market") during 2017.[5] Economist Robert Shiller says this volatility damages Bitcoin's store-of-value credibility and is a major hurdle to its acceptance as a currency.[6]

The store-of-value function has also been diminished because of hacking attacks, thefts, and other security problems.[7] For example, hackers brought down Mt. Gox, which in 2014 was the largest Bitcoin exchange, and 850,000 Bitcoins went missing at the same time (valued at $14 billion at a price of $17,000 each).[8] On December 7, 2017, hackers stole $70 million worth of Bitcoin.[9] Bitcoin owners lack the ability to hold Bitcoin as a deposit in a bank; instead, owners must hold them in a digital wallet and deposits are not government insured the way the Federal Deposit Insurance Corporation and the National Credit Union Administration insure deposits at banks and credit unions.

Money also serves as a unit of account, a common measure to value goods and services. Because Bitcoin prices fluctuate dramatically while the market is open and from day to day, retailers must recalculate their Bitcoin price frequently, which is likely to confuse both buyers and sellers. In addition, the price of Bitcoin fluctuates on exchanges, and Bitcoin often trades at different prices on different exchanges, which further complicates pricing decisions by sellers.[10] Finally, the high cost of one Bitcoin relative to the price of ordinary goods requires merchants to quote Bitcoin prices for most goods to four or five decimal places. For example, if a Bitcoin trades for $11,000, a $2 candy bar (in Bitcoin, or BTC) would be priced at 0.00018 BTC, or $1.8 \times 10{-}4$ BTC. Most modern accounting systems accommodate two decimal points in the price of a good (not five). In short, while Bitcoin is a virtual currency, it lacks some key characteristics that could render it more useful.

Is Bitcoin a Financial Investment?

The line between money and financial assets is not always clear. In fact, money is a type of financial asset—one that is highly liquid (used to make payments) but that typically pays little or no interest.[11] Other types of financial assets are less liquid but offer the potential to pay returns. For example, people buy stocks and bonds with the expectation that they will earn interest, receive dividend payments, or sell the asset at a higher price in the future. While Bitcoin was originally developed to function as currency, there has been a noticeable increase in demand from those who buy Bitcoin as a speculative investment.[12]

This speculation by investors has driven Bitcoin prices to rise so fast that some financial experts call it a "financial bubble." One definition of a bubble is when the price of an asset diverges from its underlying fundamental value. Think of a bubble you blow with bubble gum—as you blow more air into the bubble it gets bigger and bigger, but at some point the pressure exceeds the capacity of what the gum can hold, and it pops. Similarly, a financial bubble occurs when increasing demand for an asset causes its price to rise higher and higher, far above its underlying value. As prices rise, current investors enjoy rising asset prices and might be tempted to buy more. Others, afraid they are missing an opportunity, may see the upward momentum and choose to invest, assuming that the trend will continue. But bubbles often pop— that is, there is a big price drop—generating large losses for those holding the asset.

How quickly did Bitcoin prices rise? While prices fluctuated wildly during the year, Bitcoin finished 2017 with a gain that was just shy of 1,400 percent.[13] Financial experts see investors' excitement about Bitcoin as similar to investors' response to technology stocks in the 1990s and houses in the 2000s—in both cases, investors continued to buy even after prices had climbed, expecting that others would buy the asset from them at even higher prices in the future. Others, afraid they were missing out on a potential opportunity for profits, were drawn in— pushing prices even higher.

Both Jamie Dimon, CEO of JPMorgan Chase, and Warren Buffett, regarded as one of the world's most successful investors, have called Bitcoin a bubble.[14] Dimon has said that it is worse than the infamous tulip bulb bubble of the 1630s.[15] Buffett says Bitcoin is difficult to value because it's not a value-producing asset.[16] Stocks represent ownership of real capital and often provide a stream of dividend income; Bitcoin provides neither real capital nor income. Robert Shiller, the Nobel laureate economist who predicted the two biggest speculative markets in recent history (the tech-stock bubble of the 1990s and home prices in the 2000s), has also called Bitcoin a bubble.[17] Shiller even speculates on the possibility of competing cryptocurrencies replacing Bitcoin and driving its value to zero.[18]

Of course, bubbles are hard to spot while they are happening. Investors inevitably disagree about the "proper" value for an asset, and it's even harder to predict when bubbles will pop. Former Federal Reserve Chair Alan Greenspan suggested on December 5, 1996, that people were engaging in "irrational exuberance" by investing in overvalued technology stocks. His question seems applicable today: "But how do we know when irrational exuberance has unduly escalated asset values, which then become subject to unexpected and prolonged contractions?" After Greenspan posed this question, stock values continued to rise, at an even faster rate, for several more years. January 10, 2000, is generally seen as the price peak, before the tech-stock bubble burst and many investors lost considerable amounts of wealth. Only time will tell if the exuberance of Bitcoin buyers has been irrational.

Conclusion

Bitcoin has characteristics that allow it to function as money and make it a useful payment method. That is, it is relatively easy to transfer Bitcoin to other people or businesses, even for international transactions. However, other aspects of Bitcoin make it less desirable for everyday transactions, including security problems and volatile price fluctuations. The value of currency is determined by supply and demand. While the demand for Bitcoin has grown as people speculate on its future value, the supply of Bitcoin is set to grow at an inflexible, predetermined rate. As a result, as demand for Bitcoin has fluctuated, so has its price. This price volatility has undermined Bitcoin's ability to serve as a store of value. In contrast, governments often delegate the value of their official currencies to their central banks. For example, the Federal Reserve was founded to provide an "elastic currency" to ensure that it could adjust the money supply to provide price stability in the face of changing demand.[19]

Bitcoin's characteristics as a financial asset have drawn the interest of many and created the potential for financial loss. While the line between money and financial asset is not clear, people's actions often reveal the role the asset is playing in the economy. Lately, the excitement surrounding Bitcoin has been around buying it as a financial investment, not using it as money to buy goods and services. Weighing in on the issue, former Federal Reserve Chair Janet Yellen said that Bitcoin is "not a stable source of store of value, and it doesn't constitute legal tender"; in her judgement, Bitcoin "is a highly speculative asset."[20]

Notes

1 Randewich, Noel. "Winklevoss Twins Use Bitcoin to Book Space Trip." *Reuters,* March 5, 2014; https://www.reuters.com/article/us-bitcoin-virgingalactic/winkle-voss-twins-use-bitcoins-to-book-space-trip-idUSBREA241XQ20140305.

2 Yermack, David. "Is Bitcoin a Real Currency? An Economic Appraisal." No. w19747. National Bureau of Economic Research, 2013; http://www.nber.org/papers/w19747.pdf.

3 Browne, Ryan. "Big Transaction Fees Are a Problem for Bitcoin—But There Could Be a Solution." *CNBC,* December 19, 2017; https://www.cnbc.com/2017/12/19/big-transactions-fees-are-a-problem-for-bitcoin.html.

4 Franck, Thomas and Imbert, Fred. "Bitcoin Plunges 20% From Its High." *CNBC,* November 30, 2017; https://www.cnbc.com/2017/11/30/bitcoin-plunges-20-percent-from-its-high.html.

5 Shell, Adam. "Bitcoin Price: Digital Currency Had Big Swings in 2017." *USA Today,* December 30, 2017; https://www.usatoday.com/story/money/2017/12/29/bitcoin-price-digital-currency-had-big-swings-2017/988544001/.

6 Shiller, Robert J. "What is Bitcoin Worth? Don't Even Ask." *New York Times,* December 15, 2017; https://www.nytimes.com/2017/12/15/business/bitcoin-investing.html.

7 Yermack (2013, see footnote 2).

8 Lee, Timothy. "A Brief History of Bitcoin Hacks and Frauds." Ars Technica, December 5, 2017; https://arstechnica.com/ tech-policy/2017/12/a-brief-history-of-bitcoin-hacks-and-frauds/.

9 Iyengar, Rishi. "More Than $70 Million Stolen in Bitcoin Hack." *CNN Tech*, December 8, 2017; http://money.cnn.com/2017/12/07/technology/nicehash-bitcoin-theft-hacking/index.html.

10 Yermack (2013, see footnote 2).

11 Money may be in the form of currency, which pays no interest, or bank deposits, which typically pay fairly low interest on transaction accounts.

12 Cochrane, John H. "Bitcoins and Bubbles." The Grumpy Economist, November 30, 2017; https://johnhcochrane.blogspot.com/2017/11/bitcoin-and-bubbles.html.

13 Shell (2017, see footnote 5).

14 Nicklaus, David. "To Investment Pros, Bitcoin Looks Like a Classic Bubble," *St. Louis Post-Dispatch*, December 5, 2017; http://www.stltoday.com/business/columns/david-nicklaus/to-investment-pros-bitcoin-looks-like-a-classic-bubble/article_1c9a7dc5-cd31-56cd-b5f9-21ceae8c5ec4.html.

15 Oyedele, Akin. "Jamie Dimon: Bitcoin Is a Fraud That's 'Worse Than Tulip Bulbs.'" *Business Insider*, September 12, 2017; http://www.businessinsider.com/bitcoin-price-worse-than-tulip-bulbs-2017-9.

16 Johannesson, Makail. "Inside Warren Buffett's Master Class on Bitcoin, Self-Driving Vehicles—and Life." *Marketwatch*, October 29, 2017; https://www.marketwatch.com/story/warren-buffetts-master-class-on-bitcoin- self-driving-vehicles-clean-energy-and-life-2017-10-26.

17 Oyedele, Akin. "Robert Shiller: Bitcoin Is the 'Best Example Right Now' of a Bubble." *Business Insider*, September 5, 2017; http://www.businessinsider.com/bitcoin-price-bubble-shiller-best-example-2017-9.

18 Shiller (2017, see footnote 6).

19 Berentsen, Aleksander and Schär, Fabian. "A Short Introduction to the World of Cryptocurrencies." Federal Reserve Bank of St. Louis *Review*, 2018, *100*(1), pp. 1-16; https://doi.org/10.20955/r.2018.1-16.

20 Transcript of Chair Yellen's Press Conference, December 13, 2017; https://www.federalreserve.gov/mediacenter/files/FOMCpresconf20171213.pdf.

Chapter 2

Is Blockchain Too Risky to Operate on a Mass Scale?

A History of Bitcoin on the Blockchain

Axel Simon

Axel Simon works for Red Hat, an international open-source software company.

I
t isn't uncommon, when working on a new version of an open source project, to suffix it with "-ng", for "next generation." Fortunately, in their rapid evolution blockchains have so far avoided this naming pitfall. But in this evolutionary open source ecosystem, changes have been abundant, and good ideas have been picked up, remixed, and evolved between many different projects in a typical open source fashion.

In this article, I will look at the different generations of blockchains and what ideas have emerged to address the problems the ecosystem has encountered. Of course, any attempt at classifying an ecosystem will have limits—and objectors—but it should provide a rough guide to the jungle of blockchain projects.

The Beginning: Bitcoin

The first generation of blockchains stems from the Bitcoin blockchain, the ledger underpinning the decentralized, peer-to-peer cryptocurrency that has gone from Slashdot miscellanea to a mainstream topic.

This blockchain is a distributed ledger that keeps track of all users' transactions to prevent them from double-spending their coins (a task historically entrusted to third parties: banks). To prevent attackers from gaming the system, the ledger is replicated to every computer participating in the Bitcoin network and can be updated by only one computer in the network at a time. To decide which computer earns the right to update the ledger, the

"Blockchain evolution: A quick guide and why open source is at the heart of it," by Axel Simon, Opensource.com, June 28, 2018, https://opensource.com/article/18/6/blockchain-guide-next-generation. Licensed under CC BY-SA 4.0 International.

system organizes every 10 minutes a race between the computers, which costs them (a lot of) energy to enter. The winner wins the right to commit the last 10 minutes of transactions to the ledger (the "block" in blockchain) and some Bitcoin as a reward for their efforts. This setup is called a *proof of work* consensus mechanism.

This is where it gets interesting. Bitcoin was released as an open source project in January 2009. In 2010, realizing that quite a few of these elements can be tweaked, the community that had aggregated around Bitcoin, often on the bitcointalk forums, started experimenting with them.

First, seeing that the Bitcoin blockchain is a form of a distributed database, the Namecoin project emerged, suggesting to store arbitrary data in its transaction database. If the blockchain can record the transfer of money, it could also record the transfer of other assets, such as domain names. This is exactly Namecoin's main use case, which went live in April 2011, two years after Bitcoin's introduction.

Where Namecoin tweaked the content of the blockchain, Litecoin tweaked two technical aspects: reducing the time between two blocks from 10 to 2.5 minutes and changing how the race is run (replacing the SHA-256 secure hashing algorithm with scrypt). This was possible because Bitcoin was released as open source software and Litecoin is essentially identical to Bitcoin in all other places. Litecoin was the first fork to modify the consensus mechanism, paving the way for many more.

Along the way, many more variations of the Bitcoin codebase have appeared. Some started as proposed extensions to Bitcoin, such as the Zerocash protocol, which aimed to provide transaction anonymity and fungibility but was eventually spun off into its own currency, Zcash.

While Zcash has brought its own innovations, using recent cryptographic advances known as zero-knowledge proofs, it maintains compatibility with the vast majority of the Bitcoin code base, meaning it too can benefit from upstream Bitcoin innovations.

Another project, CryptoNote, didn't use the same code base but sprouted from the same community, building on (and against) Bitcoin and again, on older ideas. Published in December 2012, it led to the creation of several cryptocurrencies, of which Monero(2014) is the best-known. Monero takes a different approach to Zcash but aims to solve the same issues: privacy and fungibility.

As is often the case in the open source world, there is more than one tool for the job.

The Next Generations: "Blockchain-ng"

So far, however, all these variations have only really been about refining cryptocurrencies or extending them to support another type of transaction. This brings us to the second generation of blockchains.

Once the community started modifying what a blockchain could be used for and tweaking technical aspects, it didn't take long for some people to expand and rethink them further. A longtime follower of Bitcoin, Vitalik Buterin suggested in late 2013 that a blockchain's transactions could represent the change of states of a state machine, conceiving the blockchain as a distributed computer capable of running applications ("smart contracts"). The project, Ethereum, went live in July 2015. It has seen fair success in running distributed apps, and the popularity of some of its better-known distributed apps (CryptoKitties) have even caused the Ethereum blockchain to slow down.

This demonstrates one of the big limitations of current blockchains: speed and capacity. (Speed is often measured in transactions per second, or TPS.) Several approaches have been suggested to solve this, from sharding to sidechains and so-called "second-layer" solutions. The need for more innovation here is strong.

With the words "smart contract" in the air and a proved—if still slow—technology to run them, another idea came to fruition: permissioned blockchains. So far, all the blockchain networks we've described have had two unsaid characteristics: They are public (anyone can see them function), and they are without permission (anyone can join them). These two aspects are both desirable and necessary to run a distributed, non-third-party-based currency.

As blockchains were being considered more and more separately from cryptocurrencies, it started to make sense to consider them in some private, permissioned settings. A consortium-type group of actors that have business relationships but don't necessarily trust each other fully can benefit from these types of blockchains—for example, actors along a logistics chain, financial or insurance institutions that regularly do bilateral settlements or use a clearinghouse, idem for healthcare institutions.

Once you change the setting from "anyone can join" to "invitation-only," further changes and tweaks to the blockchain building blocks become possible, yielding interesting results for some.

For a start, proof of work, designed to protect the network from malicious and spammy actors, can be replaced by something simpler and less resource-hungry, such as a Raft-based consensus protocol. A tradeoff appears between a high level of security or faster speed, embodied by the option of simpler consensus algorithms. This is highly desirable to many groups, as they can trade some cryptography-based assurance for assurance based on other means—legal relationships, for instance—and avoid the energy-hungry arms race that proof of work often leads to. This is another area where innovation is ongoing, with Proof of Stake a notable contender for the public network consensus mechanism of choice. It would likely also find its way to permissioned networks too.

Several projects make it simple to create permissioned blockchains, including Quorum (a fork of Ethereum) and Hyperledger's Fabric and Sawtooth, two open source projects based on new code.

Permissioned blockchains can avoid certain complexities that public, non-permissioned ones can't, but they still have their own set of issues. Proper management of participants is one: Who can join? How do they identify? How can they be removed from the network? Does one entity on the network manage a central public key infrastructure (PKI)?

Open Nature of Blockchains

In all of the cases so far, one thing is clear: The goal of using a blockchain is to raise the level of trust participants have in the network and the data it produces—ideally, enough to be able to use it as is, without further work.

Reaching this level of trust is possible only if the software that powers the network is free and open source. Even a correctly distributed proprietary blockchain is essentially a collection of independent agents running the same third party's code. By nature, it's necessary—but not sufficient—for a blockchain's source code to be open source. This has both been a minimum guarantee and the source of further innovation as the ecosystem keeps growing.

Finally, it is worth mentioning that while the open nature of blockchains has been a source of innovation and variation, it has also been seen as a form of governance: governance by code, where users are expected to run whichever specific version of the code contains a function or approach they think the whole network should embrace. In this respect, one can say the open nature of some blockchains has also become a cop-out regarding governance. But this is being addressed.

An All-Digital Currency Still Needs a Bank

Aleksander Berentsen and Fabian Schär

Aleksander Berentsen and Fabian Schär are both researchers for the Federal Reserve Bank of St. Louis.

I n Berentsen and Schär (2017), we argue that Bitcoin links several technological components together in such a way that the units of value are issued under competition and have both a virtual representation and a decentralized transaction process. In this way, the Bitcoin system has created money that is substantially different from any other money—such as commodity money, cash, or electronic money.

To understand why Bitcoin is unique, it is useful to characterize money according to its control structure.[1] There are three dimensions. The first dimension is representation. Money can be represented in virtual form or physical form. The second dimension is transaction handling. Money can be transacted in centralized or decentralized payment systems. Finally, the third dimension is money creation. Some monies are created by a monopoly, while others are issued under competition.

Cash is represented by a physical object, usually a coin or bill, meaning that its value is inseparable from the object. The holder of a cash unit is automatically the owner of the corresponding value. As a result, the ownership rights to the cash units, circulating freely in the economy, are always clearly defined without anyone having to keep records. This feature allows for a decentralized payment system where cash can change hands between two agents without the involvement of a third party. In most countries, the central bank or the treasury is the monopoly issuer of cash.

Commodity money, such as gold, is also represented by a physical object; and, again, the current holder of a unit is by default

"The Case for Central Bank Electronic Money and the Non-Case for Central Bank Cryptocurrencies," by Aleksander Berentsen and Fabian Schär, Federal Reserve Bank of St. Louis, February 28, 2018. Reprinted by permission.

assigned ownership of the value unit and so no recordkeeping is needed to use it as a payment instrument.[2] Gold differs from cash by its competitive creation process because anyone can enter the business of extracting gold and thereby create new gold units.

Commercial bank deposits are virtual money. Virtual money has no physical representation. It exists only as a record in an accounting system. When a payment is made, the accounts are adjusted by deducting the payment amount from the buyer and crediting it to the seller. In most countries, households and firms use commercial bank deposits to make electronic payments. There are many ways to initiate payments; the most common are credit cards, debit cards, checks, and online banking. Commercial banks compete for deposits; that is why we consider the creation of money in the form of commercial bank deposits as competitive.[3] The banks are responsible for keeping records so any transaction between a buyer and a seller requires a commercial bank or several commercial banks to update the respective accounts. For that reason, commercial bank deposits are transacted in a centralized payment system.

Central bank electronic money is also virtual money. In most countries, public access to electronic central bank money is restricted. In Switzerland, for example, it can be held only by a few financial intermediaries. As of now, there are roughly 200 intermediaries that have accounts at the Swiss National Bank and they use the funds in these accounts for settlement purposes and to fulfill reserve requirements.[4] A proposal that we label "central bank electronic money for all" would allow all households and firms to open accounts at central banks, which then would allow them to make electronic payments with central bank money instead of commercial bank deposits. (We will come back to this proposal in the next section.) Central bank electronic money is issued monopolistically and transactions are conducted in a centralized payment system.

Bitcoin is the first virtual money for which ownership rights to the various monetary units are managed in a decentralized network.

There is no central authority, no boss, and no management. And yet it still works. The Bitcoin blockchain is the decentralized accounting system, and the so-called miners are the bookkeepers. This article won't provide a detailed explanation of this mechanism; see Berentsen and Schär (2018) for that. However, we would like to emphasize that decentralized management of ownership of digital assets is a fundamental innovation. It has the potential to disrupt the current payment infrastructure and the financial system. In general, it could affect all businesses and government agencies that are involved in recordkeeping.

The special feature of cryptocurrencies is that they combine the transactional advantages of virtual money with the systemic independence of decentralized transaction processing. Furthermore, as with gold, the creation of new Bitcoin units is competitive. Anyone can engage in the creation of new Bitcoin units by downloading the respective software and contributing to the system. In practice, however, a few large miners dominate the mining process. The reason is that competition has become fierce and only large mining farms with highly specialized hardware and access to cheap electricity can still make a profit from mining (Berentsen and Schär, 2018).

The Case for Central Bank Electronic Money

Each form of money has its benefits and drawbacks. This is why many forms of money coexist. The benefits of cash are that the user can remain anonymous and there is a permissionless access to the cash payment system. In particular, users do not need to open bank accounts to use cash. Furthermore, the decentralized nature of cash transactions makes the cash payment system very robust. It is not possible to destroy it by attacking the payment infrastructure, and people do not need to fulfill any prerequisites to participate. In contrast, centralized payment systems are vulnerable: If the centralized payment processor is attacked, the entire system can come to a halt.[5]

Cash has another important benefit. With cash there is no credit relationship. Any debt is immediately settled. Therefore, there is no counterparty risk, transactions are final, and people can engage in trade even if they do not trust each other.[6] In contrast, today's electronic money (sight deposits issued by commercial banks) involves counterparty risk. Commercial bank deposits are a ledger-based virtualization of claims to physical monetary units (cash). This simply means that bank deposits are a liability of the issuer and bank customers holding bank deposits are offering a credit to their respective bank. Cash has the disadvantage that the buyer and the seller have to be physically present at the same location, which makes its use impracticable for online commerce. The benefit of virtual money such as commercial bank deposits is exactly that it allows for payments among agents that are physically separated. As such, virtual money enables new business opportunities.

Cash is also the only *liquid* asset for saving outside of the private financial system. By liquid we mean an asset that can be directly exchanged for goods and services. Gold, for example, is also a means for saving outside of the private financial system. However, according to our definition, it is not liquid because it cannot be exchanged directly for goods and services (in most cases).[7]

We believe there is great demand for a virtual asset issued by a trusted party that can be used to save outside of the private financial system. To underpin this claim, we track Swiss francs in circulation (in the form of cash) as a fraction of GDP from 1980 until 2017. We can distinguish three phases. The first phase is from 1980 until 1995, when financial innovations replaced the use of cash as a medium of exchange or store of value. The Swiss population increasingly started to use debit and credit cards for payments. The second phase is from 1995 until 2008, when card payments and online banking further expanded but the use of cash did not decline further.

From 2008 until 2017, we see a rapid increase of cash in circulation. We strongly believe that one reason for this increase is the financial crisis of 2007-08 and the subsequent euro crisis. As discussed in Berentsen and Schär (2016), the financial meltdown of 2007-08 and the euro crisis triggered massive interventions by central banks and sharply increased debt-to-GDP ratios in many countries. These events diminished the trust in the financial system, in central banks' ability to function as lender of last resort, and in governments' ability to prevent another financial crisis without having to resort to drastic measures such as confiscatory taxes or forced conversions (as represented by the Greek euro exit discussion).[8]

After 2008, the demand for cash increased rapidly since it was the only means of holding Swiss francs without facing counterparty risk. Cash was used as an insurance against the insolvency of financial institutions. For example, during the financial crisis, UBS, the largest bank in Switzerland, had to be rescued by the government and the Swiss National Bank.

We believe that there is a strong case for central bank money in electronic form, and it would be easy to implement. Central banks would only need to allow households and firms to open accounts with them, which would allow them to make payments with central bank electronic money instead of commercial bank deposits. As explained earlier, the main benefit is that central bank electronic money satisfies the population's need for virtual money without facing counterparty risk.[9] But there are additional benefits.

Cash Has Many Advantages, But Its End Might Be Near

There are political and technological reasons why the use of cash may be diminishing. Cash is being condemned by many politicians and economists. According to Berentsen and Schär (2016), the argument of these cash critics essentially is based on three claims: First, the use of cash is inefficient and significantly more expensive than electronic payments. Second, cash promotes crime and facilitates money laundering and tax evasion.[10] Third, cash hinders monetary policy by limiting the central bank's ability to use negative nominal interest rates as a policy option.

Technological reasons also apply: In the near future, a close cash substitute will be developed that will rapidly drive out cash as a means of payment. A contender is Bitcoin or some other cryptocurrency. While cryptocurrencies still have many drawbacks, such as high payment fees, scaling issues, and poor adoption, these issues could rapidly disappear with the emergence of large-scale off-chain payment networks (e.g., Bitcoin's lightning network) and other scaling solutions.

If the use of cash is restricted for political reasons or vanishes because of technological innovations, the somewhat strange situation arises that households and firms have no access to legal tender. Today, in most countries, the population can pay only with legal tender through the use of cash. If cash disappears, the population is forced to make all payments with private money. By offering transaction accounts, central banks enable the general public to hold legal tender in electronic form. A large part of the population will consider it a close substitute for cash, and this will make it easier to say goodbye to cash.

"Central Bank Electronic Money for All" Increases the Stability of the Financial System

We believe this because we conjecture that "central bank electronic money for all" would have a disciplining effect on commercial banks.[11] To attract deposits, they would need to alter their business model or to increase interest rate payments on deposits to compensate users for the additional risk they assume. The disciplining effect on commercial banks will be reinforced by the fact that, in the event of a loss of confidence, customers' money can be quickly transferred to central bank electronic money accounts. In order to avoid this, the banks must make their business models more secure by, for example, taking fewer risks or by holding more reserves and capital, or they must offer higher interest rates. This simplicity of moving funds to central bank accounts has the potential to create additional volatility. For example, there could be rapid shifts of large quantities of money from commercial bank deposits to central bank accounts that have no real causes (bank panics that are unrelated to fundamentals). In this case, the central bank is called upon to provide commercial banks with the necessary temporary liquidity by offering standing facilities where commercial banks can obtain central bank money against collateral in a fast and uncomplicated way.

"Central Bank Money for All" Simplifies Monetary Policy and Makes It More Transparent

The central bank could simply use the interest rate paid on these accounts as its main policy tool. If markets are not segregated, meaning that everyone has access to electronic central bank money, the interest rate on these accounts would be the lowest interest rate in the economy. The reason is that central bank electronic money will be the most-liquid asset in the economy and holders of such money face no counterparty risk since a central bank cannot become illiquid. Many central banks are currently discussing the possibility of normalizing interest rates. Because of the massive amount of liquidity created in response to the financial crisis, standard instruments such as open market intervention are ineffective and all instruments that are currently discussed have the characteristic that the central bank pays, in some form, interest on reserves (see Berentsen, Kraenzlin, and Müller, 2018). There is a political economy issue with these payments since, as of today, they are paid only to the few financial intermediaries that have access to central bank electronic money. The general public might not consider such large payments equitable or beneficial, and there is a high risk that it will trigger political controversies that have the potential to affect central bank independence (see Berentsen and Waller, 2014). Central bank electronic money is an elegant way of avoiding possible political upheavals with regard to these interest payments, by allowing the whole population to have access to these interest payments and not just a small group of commercial banks.

"Central Bank Money for All" Requires Low Administrative Effort

Overall, we believe that implementing "central bank electronic money for all" is straightforward since these accounts can be used only for making payments. No credit can be obtained, and so almost no monitoring is needed. (Of course, some standard regulations would still apply.) All transactions would need to be initiated electronically. Furthermore, many central banks already have a payment infrastructure in operation. For example, the Swiss National Bank already maintains one for its employees. Central bank electronic money for all would imply scaling the existing infrastructure to allow for additional account holders. However, it is not necessary that a central bank provides the infrastructure itself. Legislation could mandate that commercial banks open at least one central bank money account for each of their customers. This would allow customers to use their existing online banking access to initiate transactions from their central bank money account. These accounts would have to be maintained by commercial banks outside their balance sheets. As a result, they do not count as part of a bank's assets in the event it goes bankrupt.

This idea is related to but differs in important ways from the Chicago Plan.[12] One key element of the Chicago Plan was to eliminate the fractional reserve system by imposing 100 percent reserves on commercial bank deposits. "Central bank money for all" does not eliminate the fractional reserve system. It only amends it by requiring that all agents have access to central bank electronic money. Commercial banks can continue to offer bank deposits, and no one is forced to use central bank electronic money.

There are many open questions that need to be carefully discussed before this proposal can be implemented. In the case of Switzerland, for example, a decision would have to be made about who may hold an account at the Swiss National Bank. Is it only the Swiss population or can people living abroad have such an account? As a first step, it would make sense to narrowly define the group of users to first gain experience running the system. Furthermore, it would be wise initially to add a cap to limit the amount of money that can be held in these accounts. The benefit of such a cap is that it would allow the Swiss National Bank to gain experience, in particular, with the instruments that need to be in place to refinance the private banking system in case of large-scale bank runs.

The Non-Case for Central Bank Cryptocurrencies

The distinguishing characteristic of cryptocurrencies is the decentralized nature of transaction handling, which enables users to remain anonymous and allows for permissionless access. In this section, we argue that it makes little sense for central banks to issue cryptocurrencies even though it would be straightforward from a technological point of view to do so.

In theory, a central bank could easily introduce a central bank cryptocurrency. There exist standards such as Ethereum's ERC20 or ERC223 token standards that can be used to create new fungible tokens that are compatible with the Ethereum blockchain's infrastructure. Alternatively, one could attach additional value components to fractions of existing cryptoassets, such as Bitcoin. The additional value—in this case, fiat currency—would then be part of a specific fraction of a Bitcoin (or more precisely an unspent transaction output) and could be represented and traded on the Bitcoin blockchain. This is usually referred to as "colored coins." Finally, a central bank can develop a brand new blockchain. All approaches are fairly straightforward to implement and would allow for the issuance of a central bank cryptocurrency on a public blockchain.

To ensure parity between a crypto fiat unit and central bank reserves, the central bank must be willing to buy and sell any number of these tokens at par. The valuation will depend on the central bank's credibility; but, if a central bank is determined to issue a central bank cryptocurrency, it would have the means to do so. In fact, the convertibility mechanism can be compared with different denominations of cash, where central banks make a similar claim.[13]

However, the key characteristics of cryptocurrencies are a red flag for central banks. That is, no reputable central bank would have an incentive to issue an anonymous virtual currency. The reputational risk would simply be too high. Think of a hypothetical "Fedcoin" used by a drug cartel to launder money or a terrorist organization to acquire weapons. Moreover, commercial banks would rightfully start asking why they have to follow KYC ("know your customer") and AML ("anti-money laundering") regulations, while the central bank is undermining any effects of this regulation by issuing an anonymous cryptocurrency with permissionless access. Moreover, cryptocurrency is still a very young technology and there are large operational risks. Overall, we believe that the call for a "Fedcoin" or any other central bank cryptocurrency is somewhat naïve.

Once we remove the decentralized nature of a cryptocurrency, not much is left of it. Virtual money that is centralized and issued monopolistically by a central bank is electronic central bank money. It is worthwhile to mention that electronic central bank money could have been offered a long time ago. The technology for issuing virtual money in a centralized way existed long before the invention of the blockchain. But calling such a centralized form of virtual money a cryptocurrency is misleading.

Conclusion

The distinguishing characteristic of cryptocurrencies is the decentralized nature of transaction handling, which enables users to remain anonymous and allows for permissionless access. These key characteristics are a red flag for central banks, and we predict that no reputable central bank would issue a decentralized virtual currency where users can remain anonymous. The reputational risk would simply be too high. Rather, central banks could issue central bank electronic money. This money would be tightly controlled by them, and users would be subject to standard KYC ("know your customer") and AML ("anti-money laundering") procedures.

Some central banks supposedly are evaluating the issuance of a central bank cryptocurrency. However, a closer look at these projects reveals that these are not cryptocurrencies according to our definition. The projects usually are highly centralized.

In general, we don't think that a central bank should be in the business to satisfy the demand for anonymous payments. We believe that such a demand can and will be perfectly satisfied by the private sector, in particular through cryptocurrencies. History and current political reality show that, on the one hand, governments can be bad actors and, on the other hand, some citizens can be bad actors. The former justifies an anonymous currency to protect citizens from bad governments, while the later calls for transparency of all payments. The reality is in between, and for that reason we welcome anonymous cryptocurrencies but also disagree with the view that the government should provide one.

Notes

1 We focus on Bitcoin, but many other cryptocurrencies share similar characteristics. However, more than 1,500 cryptocurrencies have come into existence in the past few years and some do not feature all the characteristics that we find essential to be qualified as a cryptocurrency (see Figure 1).

2 We abstract from the case where an agent holds a unit of gold and is not the legal owner, such as a bank that keeps gold for its customers in a vault.

3 In some countries, competition for commercial bank deposits is restricted by financial regulations. For these countries, commercial bank deposit creation lies somewhere between monopoly and competition (see Figure 1).

4 For that reason, electronic money issued by the Swiss National Bank is called reserves.

5 A centralized payment infrastructure has many more disadvantages: Plenty of user data are collected, users can be locked out of the system, and their funds can be confiscated, which is all too often the case in countries with dubious legal systems. Furthermore, centralization may lead to a systemic dependence and rent-seeking behavior. Additionally, vendors are in constant fear of chargebacks.

6 Like cash, Bitcoin is not a liability and, therefore, holding Bitcoin involves no counterparty risk.

7 In the finance literature, there are many competing definitions for the term "liquid asset." We use the one developed in the literature labeled "new monetarist economics" (e.g., Williamson and Wright, 2010) and "search theoretic approach to monetary economics" (e.g., Nosal and Rocheteau, 2011; Kiyotaki and Wright, 1993).

8 As discussed in Berentsen and Schär (2016), cash is an insurance against bad outcomes by enabling its holder to remain "liquid" when disaster hits. Financial crises (e.g., the Lehman collapse), confiscatory taxes (e.g., Cyprus and Argentina), or (anticipated) forced conversion (e.g., Grexit, Argentina) are just a few examples of recent events in which holding cash was advantageous. The rapid increase in cash in circulation in Switzerland after the financial crisis cannot be explained only by low interest rates, since Switzerland already had a spell of zero interest rates shortly after the year 2000 when no such increase occurred.

9 A holder of electronic central bank money faces no counterparty risk because a central bank can always print its own liabilities. In contrast, commercial demand deposits are a promise to pay out cash (central bank money) on demand and that promise might not be fulfilled. However, central bank money is not immune to financial disaster. Historically, hyperinflation has impoverished many households that have held a large part of their wealth in the form of cental bank currency (see Berentsen and Schar, 2016).

10 There are many politicians and economists (e.g., Rogoff, 2016) who want to abolish cash because they believe that it is mainly used for criminal activities, money laundering, and tax evasion. If this argument is true, then the Swiss population became less criminal during the 1980s, and then its desire for crime stabilized during the 1990s, and finally, from 2007 on, the Swiss franc was used to conduct more money laundering and tax evasion (see Figure 2). It should be clear by now that we are not convinced by this argument.

11 Note that we believe that central bank electronic money for all will increase the stability of the financial system. In fact, there is a need for research that quantifies the effects of this mechanism on the stability of the financial system.

12 The Chicago Plan was developed during the Great Depression by many leading US economists. It advocated a major monetary reform including 100 percent reserve balances to back commercial bank deposits (see Benes and Kumhof, 2012). A system with 100 percent reserve requirements is essentially identical to a system where commercial banks are forced to hold all deposits in accounts that are separated from their own balance sheet.

13 The most straightforward way to fix the exchange rate would be to offer two standing facilities. For example, assume the Swiss National Bank decides to issue a Swiss franc crypto token on the Ethereum blockchain. To keep the value of this crypto token at par, it would offer a buying facility and a selling facility. At the buying facility, it would promise to buy unlimited amounts of Swiss franc crypto tokens at, say, 0.999 Swiss francs. At the selling facility, it would offer to sell Swiss franc crypto tokens at, say, 1.001 Swiss francs. If these facilities are credible, the value of the Swiss franc token will remain between 0.999 and 1.001 Swiss francs forever. In fact, these facilities will never be used if markets are not segregated, as shown in Berentsen, Kraenzlin, and Müller (2018) for the Swiss money market.

Blockchain Is As Good As Gold, and That's a Problem

Bruno Skvorc

Bruno Skvorc has master's degrees in English language and literature and computer science and has studied blockchain since 2015.

When the idea of bitcoin was being put to paper, its author—Satoshi Nakamoto—wanted the mining of this cryptocurrency to simulate the mining of precious metals like gold. This is done by giving a reward of a certain amount of bitcoins to the miner who confirms a block.

In the beginning, the reward was 50 BTC. Every 210,000 blocks, the reward would become half the previous amount. This event is called *the halving*. After 64 halvings, the reward is programmed to be zero. If a block is mined every 10 minutes, it is calculable that the last of the 21 million bitcoins will be mined in 2140.

Comparison to Gold

Back in the 1800s, the gold rush started very rapidly. The mining was happening through generations and generations, however. This prevented the accumulation of enormous amounts of gold with certain individuals, and stopped a too early or too quick rise in price. This resulted in less HODL mentality (the mentality of not spending and waiting for the value to rise). In fact, most of the gold diggers from the early days immediately spent their gold—they needed land, tools for more digging, food, horses, gambled, drank a lot, etc. Gold was not a currency in and of itself. The real currency were the bonds, the IOUs that banks gave out to individuals in exchange for keeping their gold safe, as we've already mentioned in the cryptocurrency intro post.

"Is Bitcoin Finite or Is It Just a Myth?" by Bruno Skvorc, Bitfalls, September 17, 2017. Reprinted by permission.

As more and more gold was dug out and more and more governments started to stockpile it as a national reserve, less and less gold was available in the open market, thus increasing the price with the rising demand. A new gold vein find is incredibly rare these days and the amounts being mined are trivial compared to those from the early days—a situation comparable to how the bitcoin landscape could look in 2100.

The "work" that's a parallel to the hard work of mining the gold from an underground cave or filtering it out of a river is the "proof of work" concept we explained in the blockchain post—the process of performing thousands upon thousands of calculations by spending enormous amounts of electricity in order to *seal* a block. This is how Satoshi intended to inherently compare the two systems (gold and bitcoin):

- finite amount (new gold is not being created, only found, and the amount we'll ever find is limited)
- harder and harder to mine (calculations becoming ever more complex, and more computing power is required)
- increasingly smaller rewards
- increasingly more valuable rewards

Simulating precious metals as a means of preventing inflation in this new system of digital currency was a fundamentally good idea. However, the explosive initial growth (a theoretical maximum of 21 million coins and simply giving away thousands in the beginning) was an elementary mistake. The first miners didn't find minted gold bars in an open meadow, ripe for just picking them up and taking them to a bank. They still needed to work for them. The exponential growth of the financial complexity involved in obtaining bitcoin (increase in price, electricity demands, special chips called ASIC without which mining makes no sense these days, etc.) practically guaranteed the forming of a new 1% class. Those who now have even just one bitcoin already have more than the vast majority of people in the world will ever have, once the technology reaches the undeveloped third world countries. Why?

Not because of bitcoin's rarity or its price increase, but because it's not finite in the true sense of the word.

"What do you mean?", you may be thinking. "What about the 21 million mark?"

Finality

Every bitcoin in existence is currently split into 100 million parts. Think of them like cents to the dollar, only going into 100 million, not just 100 parts. One such part is called a Satoshi, after bitcoin's creator. But, just like the *halving* itself, this fragmentation is programmed into the code of bitcoin. The miners—the programs running the bitcoin blockchain and confirming transactions— are those in charge of enforcing those code rules. The amount of bitcoin in the world will soon start decreasing. People will lose their private keys and lose access to their wallets forever, they'll send money to the wrong address that doesn't belong to anyone, governments and corporations will stockpile it instead of spending, etc. Because of this deflationary nature (among other factors), the value of bitcoin is going up over time and will eventually reach the level at which even a single Satoshi will be too valuable to transact with. What then?

All we need to do to switch bitcoin from a deflationary into an inflationary currency or to move in the other direction and just split Satoshis further into even smaller parts is change the source code. If enough miners (the 51% majority) agree to activate this new software instead of the old one, this can happen. There is no central authority to veto the decision, there is no one to say "no, that's not bitcoin's original vision", other than the miners. This is when a so called *hard fork* happens: the splitting of bitcoin into two branches.

One branch will keep mining with the old, original software, but the other will adopt the new rules and claim that these controversial changes are needed in order for the currency to continue working. A similar thing happened recently—perhaps you've heard of two types of bitcoin existing now: Bitcoin Cash and Bitcoin Core.

But a majority (51%) is a huge number, isn't it? Surely it's not possible? Well, yes, 51% is more computing power and electricity than a single person can imagine. But if we take into account that China currently has over 70% of the bitcoin mining power and that Russia is handing out surplus electricity for state sponsored mining, the danger of them joining forces and just deciding that no more bitcoin halvings will happen is very, very real.

What we're basically saying here is that anything that can be split into an infinite number of smaller parts is not finite. *"But gold can also be split into smaller flakes, and a gram of gold is now worth as much as a kilogram used to be!"*, sceptics of this theory will often claim. That's true, but the splitting of gold stops at an atom. Even if we reach the point at which an atom of gold is worth as much as a gram is today, we can't go smaller than that. Gold really is finite, because the amount of splitting we can do is finite. Don't you think governments would split gold into infinitely smaller parts to inflate the value and make their stockpile seem more valuable if this were possible? Those who hold even a miniscule amount of gold would, in such a case, become richer by a factor of X, if X is the difference in value between the newest smallest part and the oldest smallest part's value.

Deflation Spiral

The situation in which a currency keeps increasing in relative value when compared to the goods one can purchase for it is called a deflationary spiral.

When this happens, all the users of said currency are inherently encouraged to save and stockpile it because the chances of the currency doubling in value in a short timespan are great. If there's a chance for you to get a car for one bitcoin today, or two cars for one bitcoin next week, you certainly won't spend the bitcoin, will you? The Austrian school of thought is an economic opinion which states that a deflationary spiral cannot happen or won't have a major effect because as the value of a currency starts rising uncontrollably, the cost of production for goods will proportionately drop, keeping profit margins the same across time. A followup theory states that due to this system implicitly causing lower interest rates due to encouraged saving, savers will instead be encouraged to invest into businesses and ventures, keeping the economy healthy. Bitcoin maximalists (bitcoin users who refuse to accept the downsides of bitcoin) will often list these arguments in defense of the currency. Here's why it's folly.

When the value of a currency rises relative to the price of goods we can buy for it, the users of that currency are inherently encouraged to *only* stockpile it and spend only the bare minimum they need to survive or invest. Furthermore, claiming that costs of production will drop proportionately to the rise of the value of a digital currency with a limit of 21 million on a planet of 8 billion is nonsense. There is no conceivable scenario in which the production of, for example, food will drop as much as bitcoin is rising, even with full automation of production.

And finally, it's worth realizing the biggest problem of all: in its attempt to bring us a decentralized currency, bitcoin caused an unbalance the likes of which we've never seen before. Let's re-iterate: Those who currently own even one BTC have more than 99% of humanity will ever have when (and if) this technology reaches the most undeveloped of countries.

How do we solve this? Do you think this is a problem? If so, how do we proceed and make the best of it?

The Future of Cryptocurrencies Is Uncertain

Richard Partington

Richard Partington is the economics correspondent for the Guardian.

Bitcoin is the fastest-growing asset in the world this year, but the virtual currency does not appear to have many users in London's tech district. It has been more than a month since bitcoin was used to buy a flat white or craft beer sold at the Old Shoreditch Station, according to the hospitality manager at the east London bar.

Louis Chauvin admits he cannot find the iPad that is used by staff for processing bitcoin payments, as he resumes serving customers queueing to pay with their contactless bank cards. Although the establishment sits in the capital's buzzing tech hub, and is advertised online as one of the few retailers in London accepting the hipster-cum-computer nerds' currency, as few as 20 people have asked to pay with it in the two years he has worked there.

Over the same period, the value of a single bitcoin has rocketed from around $300 to more than $11,000 this week. On Friday, the currency was trading at $10,700.

Chauvin says bitcoin's increasing value—and media coverage — has not escaped customers. More people have come in asking how it works, thinking of using it in their own shop, rather than actually paying with it, he says, adding: "It's cool, it attracts some people. But for now it's niche."

Bitcoin is a digital currency, also known as a cryptocurrency, that emerged after the financial crisis and is not underpinned by a central bank. It allows people to bypass banks and traditional payment methods for goods and services—an idea that has evidently caught the imagination of some investors, because its price has surged by more than 900% in 2017. Bitcoin—created by "miners" who use high-powered computers to solve complex mathematical problems—must be stored online using a digital wallet, and can be bought or sold using exchanges such as Bitstamp, Bithumb and Kraken.

But as bitcoin hits the stratosphere, there are fears an economic bubble is forming as it becomes treated less like a currency and more like a store of value, open for speculators making ever increasing bets on how far it can rise. Central bankers, who had to step in when the subprime mortgage bubble burst, have also warned of its dangers.

Economists have compared bitcoin's meteoric rise with past bubbles, such as the tulip mania of the 17th century and the dotcom bubble that began in the late 90s with the Nasdaq index in New York and burst in 2000. Both examples foreshadow a painful collapse for a currency that has no intrinsic value to those who hold it beyond that ascribed to it by a community of owners. Should they realise the emperor has no clothes en masse, there could be a rude awakening.

Oliver White at Fathom Financial Consulting wrote that bitcoin "certainly fits the criterion" for a bubble asset. Using data stretching back to 2013, Fathom's economists compared the price of bitcoin with its historical average and plotted that against other mainstream assets—such as shares and bonds. They found the current value of bitcoin running at six times its average price since 2013. The cryptocurrency has yo-yoed with extreme volatility over the period —over the past week, the price has leapt to as high as $11,379 and plunged to $9,146 before rebounding to $10,700.

Bitcoin disciples argue its price will rise further, viewing volatility as a necessary bump on the path to even higher valuations. Fans even coined a term to describe their tactic of holding on for dear life—Hodl. A deliberate mistyped neologism—up there with noob, to mean newbie—adding to the pantheon of computer slang.

There are some rational reasons to keep calm and carrying on hodling. Serious investors are just getting interested in a market that has so far been dominated by crypto nerds and retail investors. The Chicago Mercantile Exchange (CME) is introducing bitcoin derivatives—a form of bet on the future value of the currency—which will let hedge funds into the market before Christmas.

Commentators also point out that tech stocks in the dotcom crash were worth $2.9tn before collapsing in 2000, whereas the market cap of bitcoin currently stands at $170bn, which could signal there is more room for the bubble to grow. The libertarian dream of bitcoin's creators is of a currency existing outside the traditional world of finance. But the bigger bitcoin grows and the more conventional institutions such as the CME get involved, the more chance there is of investors losing money and for regulators to intervene.

Global financial leaders such as JPMorgan boss Jamie Dimon and Goldman Sachs's Lloyd Blankfein have warned that the currency is ripe for use by fraudsters.

Ajit Tripathi of accountancy firm PwC says bitcoin's meteoric rise and its creation myth have attracted more buyers. The currency is said to have been created by a mysterious figure called Satoshi Nakamoto, although there is no proof this is actually a real person. The absence of any government or bank standing behind the currency also fuels its appeal to those unhappy with the financial system after the credit crunch.

"Bubbles are driven by sentiment and stories, and bitcoin has a great story with a lot of mystery and spectacle to it," Tripathi says. "Is bitcoin at $40,000 by the middle of next year unthinkable? It's not— but is there a logical and rational explanation for why it should be, I don't think so."

Back in east London at the Old Street roundabout, known as "Silicon Roundabout" for its proximity to so many tech startups, Ben Page-Phillips says he fears a collapse in bitcoin's value. He also accepts the currency at the independent cafe he runs with his brother, Nincomsoup, which they first opened together just before the dotcom crash 18 years ago.

The restaurant is not exposed to a bitcoin bubble because customers pay via an app that takes on the risk by instantly converting bitcoin payments into pounds on behalf of the shop. But he likes the lower cost it brings to processing sales, unlike the "crazy fees" charged by credit card companies.

"I love that it's outside the banking system, but I have concerns," he says. "You see everyone piling in and the concern is that it's going to be artificially inflated. I would treat it like a game—it's shot up so much, and what goes up must come down."

Banks Will Come Around

Michael J. Casey

Michael J. Casey is a senior advisor for blockchain research at MIT's Digital Currency Initiative.

Whether bitcoin or its imitators eventually achieve global ubiquity, they have already achieved success in one fundamental way: forcing humans to rethink their relationship with money and banks.

Cryptocurrencies weren't on the ballot during Switzerland's "sovereign money" referendum last weekend, in which Swiss citizens rejected by a ratio of three to one a proposal to end fractional reserve banking and give sole money-creation authority to the Swiss National Bank. But they were the elephant in the room.

The very presence of the crypto alternative, I believe, will eventually force economies worldwide to disintermediate banks from money, yet the direct authors of that change won't be activist voters wielding ill-conceived referenda or crypto enthusiasts voting with their wallets.

The first phase of a transition toward a true "money of the people" will be implemented by central banks themselves, striving and competing to remain relevant in a post-crisis, post-trust, digitally connected global economy.

That might disappoint adherents of the cypherpunk dream who birthed bitcoin. But the good news for those who want governments out of money altogether is that when currencies become digital—and enjoy all the bells and whistles of programmable money—they will foster more intense global competition among themselves.

When smart contracts can manage exchange rate volatility, for example, people and businesses involved in international trade will not need to rely solely on the dollar as the cross-border currency of choice. This more competitive environment will ultimately open the door to non-government digital alternatives such a bitcoin.

"Central Banks Will Jump-Start the Decentralization of Money," by Michael J. Casey, CoinDesk, June 19, 2018 (https://www.coindesk.com/central-banks-will-jump-start-decentralization-money/). Reprinted by permission.

Backlash Against CBDCs

To be sure, official enthusiasm for central bank-issued digital currency, or CBDC as it has become known, has waned somewhat as the old guard of central banking has dug in its heels.

At the Bank of England, which spearheaded research into the idea three years ago, Governor Mark Carney has lately warned of financial instability if his institution were to directly provide digital wallets to ordinary citizens—a change that would, in effect, give everyone the same right to hold reserves at the central bank as regulated commercial banks.

The Bank of International Settlements—a kind of international club for central banks—has echoed Carney's concerns, as have other officials.

This backlash, which suggests that the bank supervisory teams within central bank bureaucracies have regained ascendancy over technologists and innovators in their internal debates over CBDC, stems from a well-founded expectation: bank runs would be a real possibility.

Why hold your money at risky, friction-laden institutions paying near-zero interest when you can store at zero risk with the central bank itself and trade it automatically with other fiat digital wallet holders?

But why, also, should we care what happens to banks?

Banks Are the Problem

The only reason to promote digital fiat currencies is precisely to bypass the banks. Whether the currency is fiat or decentralized, banks are the problem. The technical, social and regulatory infrastructure upon which they operate is decades old and fraught with unnecessary compliance costs.

Banks maintain centralized, non-interoperable databases on outdated, clunky COBOL mainframes. They rely on multiple intermediaries to process payments, each managing their own, siloed ledgers that must be reconciled against each other through time-consuming fraud-prevention mechanisms.

All these inefficient systems, instituted to address the problem of trust, merely add to the cost of trust in the system.

"Why, in a digital age, can't we move money around 24/7? Because we have bad middleware, and that bad middleware is existing financial infrastructure," says Charles Cascarilla, CEO of Paxos, which is building blockchain-based trading infrastructure for the financial system.

In addition, there's the massive political risk that comes with banks' involvement in our payments system.

The reason why it was deemed necessary for governments to bail out the world's banks to the tune of trillions of dollars in 2008 was that not doing so would have thrust our highly complex payments systems into chaos. The global economy would have had a cardiac arrest. It's that threat of bringing us all down with them that gives "too-big-to-fail" banks a hold over policymaking.

Many central bankers, still smarting from the fallout from that crisis, know this is the problem. Many see real benefits in removing banks from payments and recognize that digital currencies can help. The question is how to get there without fomenting chaos.

Gradual Solutions

One solution: a phased approach over time. You don't provide CBDC to everyone at first; you start with large non-bank financial institutions, follow it up with a certain class of large corporations, then move to smaller businesses, and only make it available to individuals as a last step.

Another solution: the introduction of a unique, central bank-determined CBDC interest rate. This would be an addition to the central bank toolkit for managing money supply, which currently hinges on a combination of a policy rate imposed on banks' reserves and interventions in the two-way market for buying and selling government securities with banks.

A separate CBDC interest rate would provide a means to calibrate the flow of money between banks and digital fiat wallets, potentially within a long-term plan to gradually shift it from the former to the latter without overly disrupting the system.

As Sheila Bair, the former Chair of the Federal Deposit Insurance Corp., argued in a recent op-ed, this new interest rate tool could enhance monetary policy, as central banks could use it to either stimulate or cool the economy. By directly affecting the rate at which people's currency holdings grow, incentives to save or spend could be directly implemented.

Still, I don't see developed-world central banks rushing to do this. Their relationships to commercial banks are too entrenched. And, for now at least, it's hard for many in that system to even conceive of a monetary system that doesn't revolve around them.

But it's different for developing-world central banks. For too long those countries' monetary policy has been driven by the policies of the world's biggest central bank, the Federal Reserve. If the Fed cuts rates, foreign, inflationary money floods into their bank-centric financial systems; if it hikes rates, they face deflationary risks. In theory, a fiat digital currency could allow them to offset those forces.

Now, of course, all of this could go wrong. A new tool for profligate governments to debase their citizens' money does not look desirable. For proof, look no further than the rogue state of Venezuela and its new, centrally controlled digital currency, the petro.

Yet that may also be what ultimately gives bitcoin, or some other viable altcoin, a chance to shine, especially as Layer 2 solutions start to help with scalability and liquidity. Central banks can't put the cryptocurrency genie back in the bottle. Their potential embrace of digital fiat currencies will happen in an era when their citizens have a choice—they can shift to these new decentralized solutions, with increasing ease.

Whether they take over the world or not, the power of the market in a more open system of currency choice will mean that cryptocurrencies will hopefully play a vital role in forcing these politicized, centralized institutions to better manage their people's money.

China on the Blockchain

Patrick Coate

Patrick Coate is a research fellow at the American Institute for Economic Research.

W e have written recently at AIER about how blockchain—and bitcoin, the cryptocurrency that is one early and prominent application of blockchain technology—may be important to the future of money and exchange. In this article, I discuss how in the past few years, the center of gravity of the bitcoin world moved to China and the lessons we can draw from the resulting cycle of consolidation and regulation. This may have important implications for the future of bitcoin, as well as a being a potential challenge to the decentralization that is part of the fundamental appeal of cryptocurrencies.

Bitcoin Goes to China

Until a few years ago, almost all bitcoin trading was in dollars. Around the end of 2013, the balance began to shift to the Chinese yuan. By 2016, over 90 percent of bitcoin trading volume was in yuan, where it remained until early 2017, although recent regulations that I will discuss shortly are beginning to reverse this trend. Business Insider in January published a striking chart showing the change in bitcoin's trading volume by currency.

There are two main reasons for this reversal. First, Chinese investors became interested in bitcoin, in part because of laws in their country restricting the movement of traditional currency. Secondly, there were until recently no trading fees on major Chinese exchanges, which means once investors became interested, the no-fee structure invited a higher volume of trading. Related

"The Evolution of Bitcoin: To China and Beyond?" by Patrick Coate, American Institute for Economic Research, March 16, 2017. https://www.aier.org/research/evolution-bitcoin-china-and-beyond. Licensed under CC BY 4.0 International.

to the fee and regulation structure, bitcoin was traded as an asset and subject to capital gains taxes in both China and the US, but because bitcoin took off earlier in the US, the Internal Revenue Service may have been quicker to monitor these transactions than Chinese regulators.

Why does this matter? It is important because while bitcoin is not governed by any central bank, its development can be affected by its user base—especially if a large percentage of that base is working and making decisions as a unified group. The migration of bitcoin trading and creation to China is important not only because Chinese investors may have different priorities than Americans, but because a lot of the Chinese activity is dominated by a small number of agents, both in the exchange and production of new bitcoins.

The network of computers running bitcoin software uses a blockchain database. New "blocks" of transactions are added all the time and are linked to existing blocks. Each new block requires a computing power-intensive "proof of work" to be accepted by the network. One important feature of bitcoin is that new bitcoins are given to users who add these blocks. This is known as bitcoin "mining" and is an important way to ensure that the bitcoin network maintains significant computing power.

This system also resists manipulation because it relies on many different computers running bitcoin software. Any important changes to the system must be adopted by essentially the whole network, which allows, for example, generally accepted security patches or updates to be adopted but resists manipulation by individual actors. However, this safeguard depends on the breadth of the network.

According to a June 2016 *New York Times* article, by April of 2016 over 70 percent of bitcoin transactions were going through four Chinese companies. Almost half of newly mined bitcoins were produced by just two mining pools, or groups that pool resources and share the successfully mined bitcoins. This creates the potential for market power, in which a small group could unilaterally impose changes on the network. In the worst case, this could create a "hard fork," in which competing protocols would each create new blocks recognized as valid by a substantial fraction of the bitcoin network. Other users would have to gamble on which transactions would count, which could cripple bitcoin's usefulness as a store of value or medium of exchange, two essential properties of money.

This power is more than a theoretical possibility. The *Times* article also described an American delegation that came to China early in 2016 to discuss a bitcoin software proposal designed to alleviate congestion and transaction delays. While there was significant debate about the merits of the proposal, there was no doubt the Chinese companies had the ability to tip the scales by choosing to endorse or reject the proposal.

This can be a dangerous precedent if the short-term incentives of a mining pool are at odds with the overall health of the system. The *Times* interviewed Bobby Lee, an executive of one of the Chinese companies. Although Lee dismissed both these concerns and the idea that the major Chinese bitcoin companies were a single bloc, other observers have warned about this possibility. As a recent article on NASDAQ.com said, "Bitcoin, the currency, and bitcoin, the system and underlying technology, are two separate things, as shown by the current emphasis to separate the technology that underlies the bitcoin blockchain from the currency. What is good for the currency is not necessarily good for the system, and vice versa." The article also quoted a former director of MIT's Digital Currency Initiative, Brian Forde, "as governments and large corporations start to adopt the bitcoin blockchain infrastructure around the world, they will have to think through the concentration of bitcoin mining that is happening in China, and maybe they will have to put up speed in doing bitcoin mining in their countries, to start to decentralize even further and increase the security."

It is clear that by 2016, China had become the center of the bitcoin world. However, the balance may be shifting away from China, in large part because of the actions of China's own central bank.

Recent Regulations

In 2017, Chinese regulators have taken a stronger interest in bitcoin, and there have been significant restrictions on the flow of bitcoins in China. In late January, the *Wall Street Journal* reported that the three largest bitcoin exchanges in China each instituted a 0.2 percent transaction fee. The article cited statements on each exchange's website indicating the change was "to further curb market manipulation and extreme volatility," and it further noted that the Chinese central bank had begun investigating the exchanges earlier in January.

In early February, it became clear that regulators were not satisfied. Many observers suggested that regulators are interested not only in curbing speculation, but in restricting the flow of money out of China. The *Business Insider* piece cited earlier pointed out that China's foreign reserves fell by 8 percent in 2016. If so, any crackdown on bitcoin exchanges is either symbolic or pre-emptive. The *Wall Street Journal* cited an estimate by Chainalysis, a start-up specializing in monitoring and protecting bitcoin transactions, that the value of bitcoins removed from China in 2016 was only about $2 billion, a drop in the bucket of the nation's roughly $3 trillion in total reserves.

According to multiple reports, regulators met with major bitcoin exchanges on Wed., Feb. 8, and warned them not to violate regulations related to issues such as money laundering and foreign exchanges. The next day, two of the three largest exchanges announced a one-month freeze on withdrawal of bitcoins, and the third announced that withdrawals would be permitted but would require 72 hours to process. (The third also halted withdrawals the following week.) All three cited concerns about illegal transactions. The market responded swiftly, and the ban was quickly followed by a 10 percent decline in bitcoin prices, to $960 from about $1,060. However, prices recovered rapidly and passed the $1,060 mark by Feb. 20. Bitcoin continued to rise and was trading at nearly $1,200 just one week after that.

The Future of Bitcoin—Money, Trailblazer or Both?

Some observers believe that these regulations are to bitcoin's long-term benefit, due to engendering trust among people who may worry about bitcoin's legitimacy. This is one possible reason for the rise in prices after the initial drop. A CNBC article quoted the CEO of a bitcoin research company saying on Feb. 10, "These marketplace changes will inevitably slow nefarious activity and open channels to more and more institutional investors. In my opinion the 'PBoC [People's Bank of China] clean-up' is the best thing that could have happened to bitcoin this year." This is obviously speculative but is consistent with the sharp appreciation in bitcoin's value in late February. As the quote suggests, the potential benefits apply to use of bitcoin as money—or more generally as a financial asset.

Indeed, both regulators and bitcoin's users in the marketplace invite the question of whether bitcoin is actually money at all. The FAQ section on bitcoin.org is very clear in describing bitcoin as digital money. In the US, the IRS declared in 2014 that virtual currencies such as bitcoin would instead be considered property.

However, the status of money is determined not only by lawmakers but by users. Bobby Lee was quoted by *Business Insider* calling bitcoin "a very ripe opportunity for day trading to make money," but he also noted that bitcoin "has not taken off in China as a form of payment." Overall, as shown in the *New York Times* article, only a small proportion of bitcoin transactions put bitcoins into individual wallets to be exchanged directly for goods and services. The vast majority of activity is on the market exchanges —people buy and sell bitcoins on the exchanges, but they spend traditional currency. Most people do not own bitcoins, and it seems many of those who do use bitcoin to store value, but not as a primary medium of exchange or unit of account.

Even some of bitcoin's most fervent supporters are hesitant to pin its future on its potential to circulate as money. In January, *Wired* quoted Olaf Carlson-Wee of Polychain Capital, "it was a big mistake that any of this was ever compared to currency." Carlson-

Wee instead focused on the conceptual framework of blockchain's ability to decentralize other processes, as Max Gulker has written about for AIER recently.

This long-term view has been around for some time. In a 2014 paper, written during the period when Chinese mining pools and exchanges were becoming a large share of bitcoin mining and transactions, Stephanie Lo and J. Christina Wang discussed "the convergence toward concentrated processing, both on and off the blockchain," and said that this concentration is a predictable consequence of the increasing computing power necessary to maintain the blockchain and mine new bitcoins. As others have before and since, they especially praised bitcoin's role in developing blockchain technology. They wrote, "the lasting legacy of bitcoin most likely lies in the technological advances made possible by its protocol for computation and communication that facilitates payments and transfers."

It may be that bitcoin will continue to evolve, retain its current dominant position among cryptocurrencies, and even gain wider acceptance as money. It is as likely to remain a niche financial asset and be remembered as people my age remember the search engine AltaVista: an early implementation of a revolutionary idea, but not the brand name destined to gain ubiquitous acceptance. In either case, economies of scale suggest that the cycle of consolidation and regulatory attention are likely to be seen again with future cryptocurrencies or other nations in which bitcoin trading volume spikes.

CHAPTER 3

Is It Possible to Regulate Cryptocurrencies?

The Blockchain Expands

University of Cambridge Research

The University of Cambridge is one of the oldest education and research institutions in the Western world. It is located in Cambridge, United Kingdom.

More than 3 million people (three times previous estimates) are estimated to be actively using cryptocurrencies like bitcoin, finds the first global cryptocurrency benchmarking study by the Cambridge Centre for Alternative Finance.

While many members of the general public may have heard of "bitcoin", the first decentralised cryptocurrency launched in 2009, a new report from the Cambridge Centre for Alternative Finance (CCAF) paints a broader picture of "cryptocurrencies".

The report shows that cryptocurrencies—broadly defined as digital assets using cryptography to secure transactions between peers without the need for a central bank or other authority performing that role—are increasingly being used, stored, transacted and mined around the globe.

The Global Cryptocurrency Benchmarking Study gathered data from more than 100 cryptocurrency companies in 38 countries, capturing an estimated 75 percent of the cryptocurrency industry.

Prior to this research, little hard data existed on how many people around the world actively use cryptocurrencies. The conventional wisdom has been that the number of people using bitcoin and other cryptocurrencies was around 1 million people; however, based on newly collected data, including the percentage of the estimated 35 million cryptocurrency "wallets" (software applications that store cryptocurrencies) that are in active use, the CCAF research team estimates that there at least 3 million people actively using cryptocurrency today.

"Study Highlights Growing Significance of Cryptocurrencies," University of Cambridge, May 4, 2017, https://www.cam.ac.uk/research/news/study-highlights-growing-significance-of-cryptocurrencies. Licensed under CC BY 4.0 International.

While bitcoin remains the dominant cryptocurrency both in terms of market capitalisation and usage, it has conceded market cap share to other cryptocurrencies—declining from 86 percent to 72 percent in the past two years.

The study by the CCAF at Cambridge Judge Business School breaks down the cryptocurrency industry into four key sectors —exchanges, wallets, payments, and mining. Highlights of the findings are:

Exchanges

Cryptocurrency exchanges provide on-off ramps to cryptocurrency systems by offering services to users wishing to buy or sell cryptocurrency. This sector was the first to emerge in the cryptocurrency industry, and has the most operating entities and employs the most people. Currently, about 52 percent of small exchanges hold a formal government license, compared to only 35 percent of large exchanges.

Wallets

Wallets have evolved from simple software programs to sophisticated applications that offer a variety of technical features and services. As a result, the lines between wallets and exchanges are increasingly blurred, with 52 percent of wallets providing an integrated currency exchange feature.

Payments

Cryptocurrency payment companies generally act as gateways between cryptocurrency users and the broader economy, bridging national currencies and cryptocurrencies. They can fit into two broad categories: firms that use cryptocurrency primarily as a "payment rail" for fast and efficient cross-border transactions, and firms that facilitate the use of cryptocurrency for both users and merchants. The study found that the size of the average business-to-business cryptocurrency payment ($1,878) dwarfs peer-to-peer and consumer-to-business cryptocurrency payments.

Mining

In the absence of a central authority, cryptocurrencies are created by a process called "mining"—usually the performance of a large number of computations to solve a cryptographic "puzzle." The study shows how cryptocurrency mining has evolved from a hobby activity into a professional, capital-intensive industry in which bitcoin miners earned more than $2 billion in mining revenues since 2009. The cryptocurrency mining map indicates that a significant proportion of publicly known mining facilities are concentrated in certain Chinese provinces.

The study found that more than 1,800 people are now working full time in the cryptocurrency industry, as more companies are engaged across various cryptocurrency sectors.

"Cryptocurrencies such as bitcoin have been seen by some as merely a passing fad or insignificant, but that view is increasingly at odds with the data we are observing," says Dr. Garrick Hileman, Visiting Research Fellow at the Cambridge Centre for Alternative Finance (CCAF) at Cambridge Judge Business School, who co-authored the study with Michel Rauchs, Research Assistant at CCAF.

"Currently, the combined market value of all cryptocurrencies is nearly $40 billion, which represents a level of value creation on the order of Silicon Valley success stories like Airbnb," Dr Hileman says in a foreword to the study. "The advent of cryptocurrency has also sparked many new business platforms with sizable valuations of their own, along with new forms of peer-to-peer economic activity."

Blockchain Can End Money Laundering

Roy Keidar and Netanella Treistman

Roy Keidar is special counsel and Netanella Treistman is an associate at the law firm Yigal Arnon & Co.

An Israeli District Court recently ruled that Israeli banks are not obligated to provide financial services to companies whose primary business is trading in cryptocurrencies, such as Bitcoin or Ethereum. The Court reasoned that banks should not have to assume the risks associated with providing a financial platform to these digital currency businesses when the leading Israeli authorities on the subject, namely the Central Bank, the Securities Authority, and the Anti-Money Laundering and Terror Financing Authority, themselves have been struggling to delineate clear measures to minimize them.

One of the primary risks Israeli authorities and other regulators around the globe noted is the pseudo-anonymous nature of cryptocurrency holdings. Regulators view the digital token transfer method as a "black box," low in accountability and virtually impossible to subject to existing anti-money laundering (AML) and anti-terror financing regulations. However, built-in features of cryptocurrencies, specifically their underlying blockchain technology, have the potential to improve, not harm, AML efforts, even surpassing mechanisms already in place today.

The growing tension between the fast-growing cryptocurrency industry and AML guidelines is fueled by several factors, beyond Bitcoin's somewhat misguided reputation as a favorite of hackers and criminals, the primary of which is its structure. The current AML system was originally tailored to address existing centralized financial services systems. By default, these guidelines cannot account for a finance system based on intrinsic anonymity. Rather,

"How Blockchain Could End, Instead of Enable, Money Laundering," by Roy Keidar and Netanella Treistman, VentureBeat, October 8, 2017. Reprinted by permission.

AML relies on the ability to monitor and exploit the Know Your Client (KYC) process, identifying information that every financial institution is required to account for by law.

The AML monitoring mechanisms currently in place attribute every transaction to a preidentified legal entity. Data tracked in a fiat money paper-trail includes: (a) the financial system entry point, i.e. opening bank account, and (b) any transaction within the system, for example, sending money from one bank account to another or use of swift platforms. The systems then monitor the financial activity, evaluate the AML risks associated with such transactions, and follow up with any relevant notifications and reports. Use of the financial proceeds of a crime, when identified, can be easily attributed to a particular person.

Critics of cryptocurrencies point to the lack of identifying information throughout digital transactions as a substantial obstacle to existing AML surveillance and enforcement capabilities. However, all of the essential regulatory and enforcement elements — identifying parties and information, a record of the transaction, and even enforcement — can exist in the cryptocurrency system. It's all a matter of adjusting perspective.

First, a cryptocurrency accounts for the identity of its users both at the beginning and end of transactions through digital wallets. Tokens are stored in electronic wallets instead of bank accounts. Only the wallet owner has access to his or her wallet. The owner can send and accept tokens from one wallet to another by providing the identification code of their wallet to the other side of the transaction. The code itself acts as a key, eliminating the need for names or other types of identification. So while the transaction itself is seemingly anonymous, in most countries today, you need to undergo the process of KYC in order to open a new digital wallet. (Just as one example, Coinbase's legal disclaimer notes that it may check account information associated with your linked bank account among other possible background checks, and the 2017 Global CryptoCurrency Benchmarking Study asserts that all wallets converting national currency to crypotcurrency perform such checks.) So by virtue of owning a digital wallet, even without necessarily using it, your anonymity is compromised.

Nevertheless, in some places, you can still open a wallet without going through a proper identification process, which may allow "dirty money" into the system. "Dirty money" and other issues like coin-join and "smurfing," make it difficult to attribute a financial transaction to a specific legal entity, presenting a problem still in need of a solution.

One possibility is the expansion of KYC as a worldwide prerequisite to issuing global e-wallets, thereby prohibiting token transfer to a wallet that does not meet that standard. Considering there is only one type of entry and exit point, unlike the multiple exchange platforms available in the fiat system, cryptocurrency could conceivably enhance identity tracking capability.

This kind of solution would require consensus by key players in the industry and complementary regulation. The recent upswing in new KYC requirements for new *and* existing wallet owners internationally suggests such standardization could be crucial for ensuring the proper functioning of the growing future cryptocurrency industry.

Additionally, thanks to blockchain technology, cryptocurrencies inherently have the potential to *reduce* AML risks when compared with fiat currencies. The blockchain is an online public ledger, where each transaction is supervised, validated, and recorded as a complete transaction history.

Public ledger viewers and crypto miners are immediately notified of *any* transfer from one holder to another. Furthermore, unlike counterfeit hard currency, which governments spend significant sums trying to combat, cryptocurrencies are almost impossible to forge, as they each carry their own unique characteristics, which are verified from end to end by miners ("miners" being the computers on which individuals and mining groups are running the blockchain). Without verification of all transaction phases, including the departure wallet, the destination wallet, and the currency type and amount, the transaction is blocked instantaneously without any human supervision. In this sense, the digital trail could better serve AML regulations than the existing fiat paper trail.

The structure of blockchain is not the only characteristic of the cryptocurrency system that benefits AML efforts. Crypto miners, which act as de facto enforcement, are integral to the system as well. Once a validation is announced to the network, miners "check the math," and a block is added to the ledger only when the required number of miners has verified the transaction. Similarly, the blockchain protocol could be revised to limit transactions to KYC-verified wallets only. All transactions could be traced back to an identified e-wallet. Moreover, AML risk analysis and alert and report-generating mechanisms could be integrated within the crypto system instead of monitoring only the entry and exit points.

As cryptocurrencies gain mainstream public attention and more individuals put their skin in the game, addressing AML challenges has become crucial. At the core of the crypto system, blockchain technology's inherent characteristics offer a platform to address, if not overcome, these challenges altogether. Evidently, there will be a price associated with such a move in the form of higher transaction costs and less anonymity. But it's a price worth paying for the purpose of allowing cryptocurrencies to carry onward and change the face of money as we know it.

With the cost of global AML measures currently estimated at over $10 billion annually, the Israeli authorities as well as law and policymakers worldwide would be prudent to look before they leap, ensuring their good intentions to protect financial intuitions and citizens don't end up blocking a technology that could provide a return on investment that far surpasses the price of transitional uncertainty.

Wikipedia Is a Model for How Blockchain Can Work

Dirk Baur, Daniel Cahill, and Zhangxin (Frank) Liu

Dirk Baur is a professor of finance at the University of Western Australia. Daniel Cahill is an associate lecturer at the University of Western Australia. Zhangxin (Frank) Liu is an assistant professor of finance at the University of Western Australia.

Almost a decade after the introduction of Bitcoin, there is a lot of hype about the blockchain technology on which cryptocurrencies such as Bitcoin are based. Some claim the technology will revolutionise commerce; others are more critical in their predictions.

But the technology behind blockchain remains a mystery to many people.

A blockchain is a decentralised, distributed and open public ledger made up of a sequence of "blocks" that are "chained" via a cryptographic hash.

If that still sounds like gibberish to you, there is a popular application that shares the philosophy of the blockchain technology that can help you understand how it works: Wikipedia.

A Decentralised, Open Public Ledger

Wikipedia is a free online encyclopedia that depends on the collaborative effort of decentralised volunteer writers called "Wikipedians" who add to this constantly increasing repository of information.

Despite being based on a central database, Wikipedia is decentralised in the sense that the ability to add information is completely open and public. This freedom to add information to the database, or ledger, and the freedom to access the full history of all previous changes, is similar to a blockchain.

While traditional encyclopedias rely on scholars to provide information, Wikipedia gives this role to the public, bypassing trusted authorities.

Similarly, Bitcoin gives the role of the intermediary to the public, bypassing traditional central intermediaries such as banks.

Other Common Features

Consensus

Wikipedians contribute information with the aim of improving the quality of the existing information. If an edit on Wikipedia is not accepted by other contributors it will be changed until a consensus is reached.

If no consensus can be reached, the "edit war" is settled by an appointed authority.

The consensus in Bitcoin follows the greatest amount of work expended by the Bitcoin network consisting of "miners," and is represented by the longest blockchain.

Miners verify transactions and expend resources to complete the "proof-of-work." Once the work is complete the network will show their acceptance by linking new blocks to the existing one.

Transparency

Contributions made by Wikipedians are transparent, similar to the open and publicly accessible transaction history of any user's Bitcoin wallet stored on the blockchain.

The time-stamped history of all edits made to the Wikipedia page is visible through the "View History." Just as each Bitcoin can be traced to its inception, all prior versions and iterations of a Wikipedia entry are publicly available and show the path towards the current consensus.

The dynamic evolution of content within Wikipedia is a major difference from traditional encyclopedias, which offer a more centralised and more static repository of information.

Trust and Incentive

Both Wikipedians and bitcoin miners replace the necessity for trusted central authorities.

Interestingly, the incentive to contribute to the network differs. Wikipedians are not financially rewarded, whereas Bitcoin miners receive Bitcoin for their contributions to the blockchain.

If a miner included an invalid transaction in their block, then the cost to complete the proof-of-work would go unrewarded as honest miners would not link new blocks to the chain.

Although the opportunity to vandalise and provide inaccurate information on Wikipedia exists, the transparency of edits makes it straightforward for honest writers to identify and rectify changes.

This discourages devious attempts to discredit the information on Wikipedia since any attempt will be recorded as a time-stamped, unalterable chain of edits. A long chain of edits represents the amount of work Wikipedians have put into developing the topic. Longer chains can signal a higher quality of information.

Points of Difference

A feature that Wikipedia does not share with the classical blockchain is encryption. Because ownership and anonymity is an important feature on the Bitcoin blockchain, encryption of information is needed so that coins cannot be stolen or duplicated.

On Wikipedia there is no ownership of information, making encryption redundant.

Another key difference is synchronised, simultaneous distribution. Wikipedia is not distributed because the participants of the network do not update and store the information on their computers. If they did, it would be very costly and thus very inefficient—a major drawback of distributed systems.

Decentralisation is also inefficient as it generally takes longer to reach a consensus. But the final outcome may be better compared to a centralised system.

In other words, Wikipedia may be less efficient than a traditional encyclopedia but the final edition may be much better.

The History of Blockchain Regulation

Andrew Norry

Andrew Norry is a writer for Blockonomi, *a blockchain-focused news website run by Kooc Media.*

Bitcoin was founded on the principles of decentralization, meaning that the cryptocurrency was not regulated by the central authority in the way that a traditional (or fiat) currency would be. As Bitcoin, and the blockchain technology behind it, remains quite new and in the early stages of its evolution, authorities are still trying to get to grips with what exactly the technology is before attempting to come up with a plan about how to deal with it, especially in relation to taxation and money laundering issues.

Currently, there is no uniform international approach to Bitcoin and its legality will depend on where in the world that you reside. However, as authorities gain more experience and knowledge about Bitcoin, and the cryptocurrency industry in general, it is likely that at least a certain minimum levels of regulation will come into place in the vast majority of countries. In addition, the huge gains being made by the cryptocurrency this year has meant that authorities are feeling that urgency about regulating the sector, with over 30 global regulators having announced various approaches to cryptocurrency regulation in recent months.

What Are the Concerns?

Not long after its inception, Bitcoin had gained the attention of regulators as a result of its popularity amongst vendors and customers on the Dark Web, an area of the internet that was rife with illegal trade in items ranging from weaponry to illegal drugs. For example, the infamous Silk Road marketplace only accepted Bitcoin on its site in order to ensure anonymity for its

"An In-Depth Look at Bitcoin Laws & Future Regulation," by Andrew Norry, Kooc Media Ltd., July 2, 2018. Reprinted by permission.

customers. The infamy of Bitcoin, and the subsequent closing down of the marketplace by the FBI, to US Senator Charles Schumer explicitly referring to Bitcoin as a "surrogate currency" that enabled criminal activities.

In addition, the semi-anonymous and decentralized nature of Bitcoin meant that authorities feared that it would be used for money laundering. For example as early as April 2012 the FBI indicated that the lack of regulation could mean that Bitcoin could be used for illegal activities by criminals, especially when offshore exchanges were available.

Other issues arising include the fact that as Bitcoin has risen in value, its usefulness when it comes to making transactions has fallen and it is being used more and more to store value, leading to the possibility of a bubble. It is suggested that the vast majority of Bitcoin transactions over the last 12-24 months have been for speculation purposes, with the volatility of the asset and the demands (and resulting expense) that the sudden surge of interest has placed on the currency making it increasingly unsuitable for everyday transactions.

Current Approach to Regulation

Although a small number of countries have restricted or banned Bitcoin, most countries allow Bitcoin to be used, while a patchwork of regulations having been put in place in different countires. The decentralized nature of Bitcoin makes it very difficult to enforce restrictions on Bitcoin, even in those countries that have banned it. Below, we have a look at the approach of a number of different jurisdictions.

USA

The US does not yet have a uniform approach to the regulation of Bitcoin at a Federal or State level. The Federal Reserve does not have a policy towards the regulation of Bitcoin, although it has said that it may be a matter that they will have to consider at some point in the future, The Financial Crimes Enforcement

Network (FinCEN), an agency within the US Treasury Department, published guidelines about cryptocurrencies as early as 2013, which suggested that although using cryptocurrency for purchasing legal goods and services was not illegal, the mining or trading of bitcoin as well as the operation of exchanges on which Bitcoins are traded would fall under the label of "money transmitters " and would be subject to the same Anti-Money Laundering (AML) and Know Your Client (KYC) measures as other money service businesses. FinCEN has also been involved in an action again the Russian-domiciled BTC-e exchange for a breach of US AML laws, which was the first action taken against a non-US based exchange.

The US Securities and Exchange Commission (SEC) have yet to issue any regulations on Bitcoin or cryptocurrencies. However, they have issued a number of warnings about the volatility and risk of fraud in the sector, including a warning from the chairman of the SEC in November 2017 relating to the risks surrounding ICO's. The US Commodity Futures Trading Commission (CFTC) has designated Bitcoin to be a commodity, and although the CFTC does not regulate Bitcoin directly, it does have authority in respect of commodity futures that are directly connected to Bitcoin. For example, the CFTC recently accepted a proposal by the Chicago Mercantile Exchange to allow Bitcoin and other cryptocurrency to be cleared in the same manner as other products, which could have a major effect on the value of Bitcoin.

At a state level there have been various approaches taken by individual states, particularly in relation to the regulation of exchanges or other money transmitters. Some states, such as New York, have made attempts to make specific licensing regimes that are applicable to cryptocurrency exchanges whereas other states, such as Texas, continue to apply existing financial laws and regulations to the use of cryptocurrencies. However, the effect of this licence in New York was considered by some to be a stifling of the fintech industry's use of cryptocurrency in that state. In fact, the New York Bitlicence is currently being challenged by the Bitcoin

Foundation, who are increasingly active in lobbying against large scale regulation of the industry. The Bitcoin Foundation has stated its opinion that the US government is increasing federal and state regulation of Bitcoin in the US with a view to "control and stifle the adoption and use of so-called 'virtual currencies' such as Bitcoin."

European Union

The EU has taken a more open approach to Bitcoin than the US, as well as offering less ambiguity. Indeed, the EU already had a framework to govern the use of electronic money before the invention of Bitcoin, which was adaptable to fit cryptocurrencies such as Bitcoin.

The European Central Bank has classified Bitcoin as a "convertible decentralized virtual currency." The European Banking Authority (EBA) has advised European banks not to trade in any cryptocurrencies until a regulatory regime was put in place. In 2016, the European Parliament agreed to set up a taskforce to monitor cryptocurrencies with a view to combating money laundering and terrorism. The European Commission has further proposed that cryptocurrency exchanges and digital wallets would be subject to regulation in order to prevent tax evasion.

The current rapporteur of the first Blockchain Resolution of the European Parliament has suggested that the benefits of a framework of rules in respect of the blockchain industry would allow for companies and customers operating in the sphere to act on a level playing field. She stated that without certainty about regulation, it is unlikely that the required scalability of the technology will be able to occur. She further proposed that ICOs, for example, should be defined within their own structure, rather than any attempt be made to make it fit into the current regulatory structures of securities or commodities. This approach is in line with the view of the Bitcoin Foundation themselves, who have stated that any premature regulation of Bitcoin "might put it into a box it might not fit into later on."

China

Although legal for individuals in China, there has been a clampdown on the trading of Bitcoin in 2017, with multiple exchanges having to delay or pause Bitcoin withdrawal services. This clampdown arrived in tandem with an increase in the Chinese media noting the dangers of cryptocurrency as a tool for criminal activities, which suggests that this has been a *de facto* regulation of Bitcoin. In addition, officials in the People's Bank of China have noted that Bitcoin exchanges operating in China needed strict supervision and a form of licensing.

Tax

The other area in which authorities are increasingly looking at how regulation will be implemented in respect of Bitcoin is in the area of tax. Due to the semi-anonymity of Bitcoin, it can potentially be used to hide assets and assist in reducing taxation. There is no uniform international approach on how profits made from trading in Bitcoin or other cryptocurrencies should be taxed. For example, the EU has declared that the trading of cryptocurrencies should not be subject to VAT on the basis that the exchange transactions were a supply of services rather than a supply of goods, which is an approach that was also taken by the UK prior to the EU ruling. In the US, the IRS confirmed in 2014 that it would treat cryptocurrencies such as Bitcoin as property instead of a currency. This means that any profits made from Bitcoin investment is charged at each investor's capital gains rate as opposed to their ordinary income rate.

Future Approach

There are a number of potential approaches that authorities could take when it comes to the regulation of Bitcoin.

1. Cryptocurrency providers and exchanges will act as regulators of the currency by ensuring that AML and KYC regulations are complied with. Some of the

existing exchanges, such as Coinbase, already enforce these regulations.

2. Governments could take the nuclear option and completely block Bitcoin, or other cryptocurrencies that don't abide by government regulation. As noted above, this would be difficult to enforce as governments have thus far found it difficult to completely block access to websites.

3. Governments could alternative impose limited prohibitions, such as banning the sale of real-life goods in exchange for cryptocurrency in order to avoid Bitcoin being used as payment for illegal goods.

4. Governments could also selectively regulate the industry, especially in respect of taxation. This is similar to the current UK and EU approach. This would result in some of the fundamental areas of the industry being regulated, such as tax and AML, without widespread regulations being put in place.

5. Governments could provide supporting mechanisms whereby the consensus of users would enforce their own "community standards." The downside of this approach is that it may result in regulators allowing illegal or fraudulent activity to go unchecked.

The EU proposals for regulation have followed broadly the approach taken by the French government, which included the following proposals:

1. In order that users cannot remain anonymous, ensure that exchanges and intermediaries require proof of identity upon opening accounts.

2. Publish a set of instructions for both consumers and regulators in respect of the taxation of virtual currencies.

3. Propose caps on payments that can be made in cryptocurrencies, similar to caps that are already in place in respect of cash transactions.

4. Regulate, at an EU level, any companies that offer exchanges between cryptocurrencies and fiat currencies.

According to Steve Keen, the Head of the School of Economics, History and Politics at Kingston University in London, the regulation of Bitcoin is inevitable. He noted that the existence of a futures market in Bitcoin means that there is likely to be a drop in price due to the variety of positions that can be taken in Bitcoin. He also suggested that there are possibilities that, without regulation, hard forks could be forced upon users. He has suggested that the futures market in Bitcoin means that holders of the asset are now linked to a greater extent to the financial system, meaning that what happens in other markets can affect the price of Bitcoin.

However, across the industry there are various opinions and drivers for regulation. For some, the regulation of Bitcoin would add legitimacy to the cryptocurrency. However, for others Bitcoin is low on the priority list as it is not a pressing issues. In addition, the cryptocurrency industry itself are opposed to large scale regulation that would negatively affect the decentralized nature of Bitcoin. The other issue, as suggested above by the EU approach, is that the regulators remain unsure about what or how to regulate. Fitting the cryptocurrency industry into the existing structures is likely to stifle the industry. However, to create a new regulatory and tax structure purely for cryptocurrency like result in significant expense on the taxpayer.

The year 2017 has seen cryptocurrencies break away from being a niche industry used by the tech industry to become something far more mainstream. This breakout has resulted in Bitcoin becoming a buzzword in the office and in the home. As a result, it has become almost inevitable that regulation in some form or another is on the way. However, the big questions that remain are what form will such regulations take and what effect will they have on the industry.

Bitcoin Is Not Designed for Regulation

David Trilling

David Trilling was a staff writer at Journalist's Resource, a project of the Shorenstein Center on Media, Politics and Public Policy at Harvard University.

Bitcoin is no longer just for geeks in obscure corners of the internet. Today you can use the digital currency to fly to Britain, buy an apartment and enroll in the London Sushi Workshop. Fans like its libertarian footing, how it dodges government control and how—especially in this privacy-challenged era—it boosts anonymity. But some detractors blast bitcoin and other cryptocurrencies as a "fraud," while others argue that they fuel cybercrime.

Unlike the American dollar or British pound—which are guaranteed by central banks that set interest rates and print currency, stabilizing their value—bitcoin is decentralized. No one controls it. In part for that reason, its value has yo-yoed wildly. After more than quadrupling against the dollar between January and August 2017, bitcoin fell by a third in the first two weeks of September. Some blamed a crackdown on digital currencies in China and the "fraud" comments from J.P. Morgan Chase CEO Jamie Dimon, who compared bitcoin to the Dutch tulip bubble of the 17th century. Yet as *Fortune* magazine noted, bitcoin meltdowns have been a regular feature of its brief lifetime.

This volatility makes it unlikely bitcoin (or another cryptocurrency, such as ethereum) will become an effective store of value (like gold) or a unit of account (like the dollar) anytime soon. You wouldn't want to be paid in bitcoin, since your real (i.e., dollar-denominated) salary would fluctuate all over the place. And you wouldn't want to spend bitcoin today if you think it'd be worth a lot more tomorrow.

In this explainer, we discuss what makes bitcoin different from the old-fashioned greenback and why some governments are trying to ban it. We describe how the blockchain technology behind the system could revolutionize many other industries. And we look at how a bitcoin outgrowth known as initial coin offerings (ICOs) is testing regulators.

How Bitcoin Works

Any bitcoin transaction—let's say between a buyer (me) and a seller (the London Sushi Workshop)—creates a unique digital code that is stored in an online, open ledger known as a blockchain. Everyone has access to the blockchain, but no one can see who those buyers and sellers are unless they wish to be identified. Each has a unique, pseudonymous address for the transaction.

The London Sushi Workshop's balance, which has grown because I paid my tuition, is a series of codes, also known as personal keys. The sushi school can keep them in "cold storage"— offline on something like a USB stick—or print them out. Or the school can keep them in something called a "wallet," which is run by an online third party and, just like your physical wallet, can be stolen (or in this case hacked). When the London Sushi Workshop wants to convert bitcoins to dollars or pounds, it can make the transaction through an online exchange (also third parties, which have likewise been hacked, resulting in losses for individuals) and transfer the cash to a bank account.

This decentralization puts bitcoin beyond the reach of regulators, but also creates risks. Third parties in the "wallet" or "exchange" businesses do not offer the kind of insurance you get at a bank. And, like with cash, if you print your bitcoin codes and stash them under your bed, you run the risk of losing all in a fire or robbery.

Blockchain and Mining

An anonymous programmer calling himself Satoshi Nakamoto introduced bitcoin in a 2008 paper. The widely cited paper may be best remembered for something else, though: Nakamoto also introduced the first working blockchain, the technology underpinning bitcoin.

Blockchain is an online ledger of all transactions that's available for anyone to view and copy, but that no one individual controls. Instead, it lives on many computers, where it is constantly updating itself. This decentralization and openness ensure a transaction can't be faked—because that transaction wouldn't appear on all the other copies of the ledger. If one copy of the ledger does not match the rest, that copy will stand out. Thus blockchain is sometimes called a "distributed ledger" or "distributed ledger technology" (including by J.P. Morgan Chase, which is researching how to use it).

For the bitcoin blockchain, powerful computer networks called "miners" validate the most recent transfers, ensuring someone doesn't send money they don't have. These miners' computers compete with one another to verify and then lock the transfers onto the ledger, where they never can be changed, adding a new block of confirmed transactions about every 10 minutes.

As an incentive for constantly checking and verifying bitcoin transactions, the miner that succeeds in creating a new block is rewarded in new bitcoins that he has created. These days, the reward is 12.5 bitcoins and there are about 16.5 million bitcoins in circulation (worth, as of this writing, about $65 billion in US dollars). By design, the reward drops by half about every four years until, sometime a few decades from now, the miners have created 21 million bitcoins. The creator artificially capped bitcoin at that number, ensuring the currency cannot be debased by oversupply; the coins can, of course, be divided into smaller and smaller units.

Because the database is distributed across such a broad network, hacking it would require enormous computing power. Any would-be fraudsters with that much computing muscle would find it more profitable to mine the blockchain and create new bitcoins.

The blockchain solves the "double-spending problem" that plagued earlier cryptocurrencies, whereby someone could spend the same money in two places (or counterfeit it). Today, sending the same bitcoins to two different sellers would create a "fork" in the blockchain, immediately rendering one of the transactions invalid.

Likewise, it's not possible to alter a transaction record. To go back and change a link in the chain, you'd have to change all the links that follow. That would require more computer power than all the computers that are managing the blockchain put together. The altered chain wouldn't match; it would be a clear counterfeit.

These days, miners often work with specialized computer farms that use loads of electricity; sometimes they share resources to form "mining pools." You could run a mining application in the background of your work computer, but it likely wouldn't net you anything besides a slower computer. (For example, a farm using subsidized, coal-powered electricity in China is home to 58 percent of the world's major mining pools, according to a University of Cambridge study; the US, the second-largest host, has 16 percent.)

The Promise of Blockchain

Some researchers see blockchain as having revolutionary applications beyond bitcoin, such as trading stocks, safely storing data and managing supply chains, all without a middleman. It is a "foundational" technology, argues a 2017 paper by two Harvard Business School professors, with the potential—perhaps in decades—to render accountants, traders and even contract lawyers superfluous. Blockchain "has the potential to become the system of record for all transactions. If that happens, the economy will once again undergo a radical shift, as new, blockchain-based sources of influence and control emerge."

Initial Coin Offerings

A new trend in cryptocurrencies is the "initial coin offering," or ICO. ICOs raised $2.2 billion in the first nine months of 2017, according to one industry estimate. These are not bitcoins, but essentially a new digital currency used to fund a specific product.

ICOs work like this: A company raises capital by selling virtual coins or tokens. Perhaps these coins could be used later to participate in the project, or they offer some other future reward. But they do not offer the same rights demanded by a venture capitalist or shareholder. Indeed, though they sound suspiciously similar, an ICO is not an IPO—initial public offering (which is when a company begins selling shares to the public and becomes listed somewhere like the New York Stock Exchange). Rather, ICOs happen well outside the regulated banking industry and governments fear they encourage risky speculation.

The Securities and Exchange Commission (SEC)—the regulator of US financial assets—has warned investors that some ICOs may constitute fraud, and that some coins may in fact function like securities and need to be regulated as such. Canada's securities regulator has issued a similar statement.

Government Response

Governments don't like bitcoin much. Its anonymity allows users to operate in the shadows, sell narcotics, capitalize on ransomware (software that hijacks a computer until the owner pays a ransom in a cryptocurrency) and maybe, some fear, finance terrorists.

Plus, there are tax implications. In most countries, citizens are required to pay taxes on earnings. But the taxman can't peer into your bitcoin holdings the way he can look at your Bank of America statement (though, by law, Americans are required to pay taxes on bitcoin profits).

And finally, cryptocurrencies undermine government authority. North Korea may be using bitcoin to evade sanctions.

In September 2017, China took steps to ban cryptocurrency transactions shortly after banning new ICOs. After both announcements, bitcoin's value tumbled.

Bitcoin believers argue that the community can regulate itself. But Tim Swanson, a scholar of cryptocurrencies at the Singapore University of Social Sciences, wrote on his blog in September 2017 that the idea the cryptocurrency community can police itself ignores its users' self-interested motivations. Some users, trying to drum up demand, discount the threat posed by hackers (who exploit weaknesses in third-party systems used to store bitcoin). Others lobby against regulations because "much of the original bitcoin infrastructure was set up and co-opted by bitcoiners themselves, some of whom were bad actors from day one."

A cat-and-mouse game between regulators and bitcoiners seems likely to occupy both communities, as well as scholars and governments, for the foreseeable future. Proposals for an outright ban are unlikely to end the conversation, since, to work, any ban would require harsh punishments, says a 2017 paper in the *Journal of Economic Behavior and Organization*.

One potential solution is for governments to issue their own cryptocurrencies. A September 2017 report from the Bank for International Settlements—the Basel-based arbiter for central banks—describes some projects in the works. Sweden, for example, is thinking about using blockchain technology in some of its central bank's currency-trading infrastructure. In America, some have proposed "Fedcoin" as a government-backed crypto-dollar. Though Fedcoin may attract users, it is unlikely, suggests one American central banker, to satisfy diehard bitcoiners.

The Failure of Bitcoin Regulation

Andrea Castillo

Andrea Castillo is Program Manager of the Technology Policy Program for the Mercatus Center at George Mason University.

Last summer, the New York Department of Finance Services (NYDFS) announced plans to craft new money transmission regulations for the burgeoning cryptocurrency industry operating within its borders.

In his initial press release, Superintendent Benjamin Lawsky explicitly cited protecting "beneficial innovation" and consumers as a primary motivation behind the decision to promulgate the new regulations, known as the "BitLicense."

But as the final BitLicense rules have taken effect this month, the opposite has occurred: Bitcoin businesses large and small have been fleeing the state in droves, leaving New York residents with few legitimate ways to get involved in this white hot industry. Other states should heed New York's regrettable lesson to avoid a similar fate.

Before policymakers can develop proper oversight for a new technology, they must first understand how that technology works.

Peer-to-peer cryptocurrencies like Bitcoin create value for their users by providing a distributed currency and payment network that resists censorship by external parties. Traditional online payment systems that most of us use require a trusted third party — like Visa, or Bank of America, or PayPal — to "pull" funds from our accounts and send them to the recipient's account.

Bitcoin's technological innovation replaces such third parties with the protocol itself. Computers running the Bitcoin software contribute processing power to maintain the blockchain, a

"Hey, New York: Bitcoin Doesn't Need a BitLicense," by Andrea Castillo, Foundation for Economic Education, August 15, 2015. https://fee.org/articles/hey-new-york-bitcoin-doesn-t-need-a-bitlicense/. Licensed Under CC BY 4.0 International.

distributed ledger of all transactions that records and verifies new each new transfer.

Bitcoin, unlike traditional online payment channels, is a "push" technology: the user, and only the user, can control when and where their bitcoins go.

This technological breakthrough allows an exciting range of applications in commerce, finance, and law. Users can directly program special transactions to facilitate distributed arbitration, micropayments, and even self-enforcing "smart" property services, without the need to place trust in any one party.

In general, Bitcoin and similar technologies provides more options for consumers who may value security and control over third party maintenance and customer service. These attributes explain Bitcoin's rousing successes in payments and innovation.

In six short years, the cryptocurrency ecosystem has gone from a handle of hobbyists on Internet forums to a healthy ecosystem of competing cryptocurrencies topping $4 billion in market capitalization. Venture capitalists and legal financial institutions alike have flocked to blockchain technologies for their promise to minimize vulnerabilities and costs.

But from a regulator's point of view, Bitcoin's distributed nature presents a significant policy challenge. How can governments apply existing "know your customer/anti-money laundering" (KYC/AML) regulations to cryptocurrencies?

Normally, state and federal regulators require third party payment processors to compile detailed personal information about their customers in an effort to cut down on illicit transfers. But with Bitcoin and other cryptocurrencies, such a third party payment processor does not necessarily exist.

In this, Bitcoin is similar to cash. Users can opt to trust a third party, such as Visa or Coinbase, to manage their funds or they can transfer bitcoins or dollars directly to the recipient. Money transmission licensing policies that impose onerous requirements on direct transfers and small start-ups in an effort to regulate large payment processors run the risk of quashing promising cryptocurrency ventures before they have a chance to take flight.

The state of New York attempted to tackle this dilemma head on with the BitLicense, which was expected to provide a model for other states to copy. In retrospect, states would be wise to avoid the onerous regulations on which New York eventually settled.

The first version of the BitLicense was phrased so vaguely that mere software developers contributing to Bitcoin projects might have been required to submit laborious KYC/AML reporting intended for third party custodians.

Subsequent versions at least took into account a few of the thousands of critical comments from the public by clarifying these and other ambiguities. But plenty of confusing phrases and onerous mandates nevertheless made their way into the final BitLicense regulations that took effect last week.

The current BitLicense regulations impose near-impossible standards on small cryptocurrency startups.

To start, firms must pay a $5,000 BitLicense fee even if they already obtained a federal money transmission license indicating compliance with the same standards. This might not be a lot of money for an established financial firm, but a few thousand dollars can easily snuff out an innovative but cash-strapped start-up before it even gets off the ground.

Even then, the BitLicense fee is deceiving: one cryptocurrency executive reports that the total legal, labor, and compliance cost of securing a BitLicense exceeded $100,000 for his firm.

Additionally, BitLicense imposes weird and unnecessary requirements that cryptocurrency firms seek NYDFS pre-approval for normal business decisions about product offerings, inflicting still more costs on firms who merely want some breathing room to innovate.

While a few large, capital-rich establishments may be able to shoulder such heavy burdens and stay in business, these unnecessary and considerable BitLicense costs create an environment that is hostile to innovation and growth.

It is unsurprising that the BitLicense's early days saw a mass exodus of cryptocurrency firms from the state of New York.

Less than two weeks after the ill-fated regulations' debut, at least ten major cryptocurrency firms have announced that they are leaving the state or blocking any business coming from within New York state borders.

Even LocalBitcoins.com, a Craigslist-style directory listing in-person Bitcoin sellers in different cities, decided to ban any New York sales out of fear that BitLicense regulations could one day be used to take down their business.

The few firms that *do* successfully secure a BitLicense will be operating under stricter regulations than even traditional money transmitters. By promulgating poor regulations for the still-developing cryptocurrency industry, the state of New York has already severely limited the innovative applications that this technology will bring to other states.

Meanwhile, those who wish to use cryptocurrency to launder money in New York will find a way to do so anyway.

The preemptive BitLicense regulations resulted in the worst of both worlds: New York residents are deprived of innovative development, and criminals must still be apprehended after the fact.

There is a better way. Policymakers should take care to craft or adapt regulations with a goal of "permissionless innovation" in mind. Cryptocurrency businesses that do not perform any third party custodial services should be exempted from money transmission regulations as much as possible.

Start-up "onramps" or grace periods could be implemented to allow small businesses to innovate and grow before being subjected to onerous reporting and fee requirements. And when in doubt, observe: taking some time to monitor a state's nascent cryptocurrency trade before rushing to regulate gives policymakers more time to determine where existing regulations are adequate or fall short.

An environment of permissionless innovation affords flexibility for entrepreneurs *and* regulators: policymakers can tweak policies around the margins to better adapt regulations to the unique needs of cryptocurrency businesses and the state's citizens.

The BitLicense, in contrast, will hinder cryptocurrency innovation in New York for much time to come while problems of criminality go unaddressed. To promote innovation while protecting consumer choice, policymakers must embrace permissionless innovation.

Decentralization Prevents Regulation by a Central Authority

Alex Hern

Alex Hern is a technology reporter for the Guardian.

Digital currencies such as bitcoin have caused a financial frenzy. Alex Hern explains what they are—and whether this is the end of "real" money.

What Is a Cryptocurrency? Is It Like Bitcoin?

In a word, yes. Bitcoin was the first cryptocurrency, and is still the biggest, but in the eight years since it was created pretenders to the throne have come along.

All of them have the same basic underpinnings: they use a "blockchain", a shared public record of transactions, to create and track a new type of digital token—one that can only be made and shared according to the agreed-upon rules of the network, whatever they may be. But the flourishing ecosystem has provided a huge amount of variation on top of that.

Some cryptocurrencies, such as Litecoin or Dogecoin, fulfil the same purpose as bitcoin—building a new digital currency— with tweaks to some of the details (making transactions faster, for instance, or ensuring a basic level of inflation).

Others, such as Ethereum or Bat, take the same principle but apply it to a specific purpose: cloud computing or digital advertising in the case of those two.

What Exactly Is a Bitcoin? Can I Hold One?

A bitcoin doesn't really exist as a concrete physical—or even digital —object. If I have 0.5 bitcoins sitting in my digital wallet, that doesn't mean there is a corresponding other half sitting somewhere else.

What you really have when you own a bitcoin is the collective agreement of every other computer on the bitcoin network that your bitcoin was legitimately created by a bitcoin "miner," and then passed on to you through a series of legitimate transactions. If you want to actually own some bitcoin, there are exactly two options: either become a miner (which involves investing a lot of money in computers and electricity bills—probably more than the value of the bitcoin you'll actually make, unless you're very smart), or simply buy some bitcoin from someone else using conventional money, typically through a bitcoin exchange such as Coinbase or Bitfinex.

A lot of the quirks of the currency come down to the collective agreement about what constitutes "legitimacy." For instance, since the first bitcoin was created in 2009, the total number in existence has been growing slowly, at a declining rate, ensuring that at some point around 2140, the 21 millionth bitcoin will be mined, and no more will ever be created.

If you disagree with that collective agreement, well, there's nothing stopping you from splitting with the wider network and creating your own version of bitcoin. This is what's known as a "fork," and it's already happened multiple times in the past (that's what competitors such as Litecoin and Dogecoin are). The difficulty is persuading other people to follow you. A currency used by just one person isn't much of a currency.

What Can I Actually Do with Cryptocurrencies?

In theory, almost anything that can be done with a computer could, in some way, be rebuilt on a cryptocurrency-based platform. Building a cryptocurrency involves turning a worldwide network of computers into a decentralised platform for data storage and processing—in effect, a giant hive-mind PC (that this no longer sounds like it has much to do with "currencies" is part of the reason some instead suggest the name "decentralised apps" to cover this sector).

We've already seen proposals for YouTube clones, collectible card games and digital advertising exchanges built on top of cryptocurrencies: "x but on the blockchain" is the new startup pitch du jour, now that "Uber for x" and "x but on the iPhone" are passé. There's already Dentacoin (Yelp for Dentists but on the blockchain), Matchpool (Tinder but on the blockchain) and even Cryptokitties (Tamagotchis but on the blockchain).

In practice, however, the available uses are rather more limited. Bitcoin can be used as a payment system for a few online transactions, and even fewer real-world ones, while other cryptocurrencies are even more juvenile than that. The excitement about the field is focused more on what it could become than what it actually is.

Why Does It Matter That It's Decentralised?

At their heart, cryptocurrencies are basically just fancy databases. Bitcoin, for instance, is a big database of who owns what bitcoin, and what transactions were made between those owners.

In its own way, that's little different from a conventional bank, which is basically just a big database of who owns what pounds, and what transactions were made between those owners.

But the distinction with bitcoin is that no central authority runs that big fancy database. Your bank can unilaterally edit its database to change the amount of money it thinks you have, and it does so often. Sometimes that's to your advantage (if your debit card gets stolen and used, for instance, your bank will just return the money) and sometimes it's not (if your bank thinks you're money laundering, it will freeze your account, potentially crippling your business).

With bitcoin, no one can do either of those things. The only authority on the network is whatever the majority of bitcoin users agree on, and in practice that means nothing more than the basic rules of the network are ever enforced.

Is This All About Crime?

It is … a lot about crime. The flip side of cryptocurrencies being decentralised databases is that for most people, most of the time, there's no downside to a centralised database. If you trust the financial system to store your funds, or Dropbox to store your files, or YouTube to host your videos, then you don't need to use less efficient decentralised versions of those services.

But if you are planning to commit financial crime, store illegal downloads, or host pirated videos a decentralised version of those services becomes much more appealing. That's why bitcoin, for instance, has become the currency of choice for online drug dealers and cybercriminals demanding ransoms to restore hacked data.

"Crime" is a broad term, though. In many countries, having a political opinion contrary to that of the ruling regime is considered broadly criminal; many more limit the freedom of their citizens in ways that citizens of liberal democracies might view as unethical and inhumane. If cryptocurrencies allow those limitations to be overcome, it may technically be promoting crime, but not in the way most cryptocurrency critics mean.

You Keep Saying "Blockchain." What Does That Actually Mean?

The concept of the blockchain lies at the heart of all cryptocurrencies. It is the decentralised historical record of changes in the ownership of the asset, be it simply spending a bitcoin or executing a complex "smart contract" in one of the second-generation cryptocurrencies such as Ethereum. Whenever a cryptocurrency transaction occurs, its details are broadcast throughout the entire network by the spending party, ensuring that everyone has an up-to-date record of ownership. Periodically, all the recent changes get bundled together into one "block," and added to the historical record. And so the "blockchain"—a linked list of all the previous blocks—serves as the full and complete record of who owns what on the network.

So What Do Miners Actually Do?

They build the blockchain. How precisely they do that varies from cryptocurrency to cryptocurrency, but bitcoin is a good example: every 10 minutes or so, one miner is semi-randomly selected to do the work of taking all the transactions they've heard about, declaring them confirmed and bundling them up into one block of transactions, which they then add to the chain. In return for doing the work, the winning miner is also allowed to "print" some new bitcoin to pay themselves a reward in bitcoin, currently worth about $140,000.

Anyone can be a miner—all you have to do is run the bitcoin software in mining mode. The tricky part is being a profitable miner. The actual work of bundling the transactions together is easy, but the real expense comes from the way the winner is selected. Think of it as a raffle, where buying a ticket involves using your computer to solve a very complex, but ultimately useless, arithmetic problem. To be in with the most chance of getting that $140,000 reward, you need to solve those problems thousands or millions of times a second to enter the raffle with as many tickets as possible, and that means building specialised computers, negotiating cheaper sources of electricity, or just hacking innocent people and using their hardware for nothing instead.

How Are People Making So Much Money?

That's the $190bn question—the value of all the bitcoin in the world at the time this article was published. The short answer is "buying low, and selling high": the value of one bitcoin has increased from essentially nothing eight years ago, to $1,200 eight months ago, to a high of almost $20,000 in December and settling at $11,000 now. Anyone who got hold of enough bitcoin early enough is now really quite wealthy—on paper, at least.

The real question is why one bitcoin is worth $11,000 (and why Ethereum is worth $1,040, and why one particular Cryptokitty is worth $100,000). There, you can find two answers. The sympathetic one is that all these cryptocurrencies are, by their nature, scarce assets—only a certain amount exist in the world. If they are to be widely adopted for real-world use, then people will need to buy those scarce assets, and so their value will necessarily be higher than they are today. The current price, in that story, simply reflects the probability that any particular cryptocurrency will actually be widely used.

Is There Trouble Ahead?

There is if you take the more hostile, second answer to be correct: that collective greed has fuelled a speculative bubble that will eventually come crashing down. As people hear stories of others making money from cryptocurrencies, they buy their own—which inflates the price, creating more stories of wealth and more investment. The cycle continues until eventually the price of the underlying asset is out of kilter with reality. Eventually, the bubble bursts, and a lot of people look around to find they've lost everything.

What Next?

Takeoff

Cryptocurrencies could achieve their ambitions, and become a widely used facet of daily life. A few people will become very rich as a result, but not really more so than early investors in other foundational technologies such as computing or the internet.

Hard Landing

Or this speculative bubble could end with a crash so severe that it destroys faith in the entire sector, driving the investors out, bankrupting the miners who've spent thousands or millions on single-purpose hardware that requires a high bitcoin price to turn a profit, and leaving cryptocurrencies as a technological dead-end alongside cold fusion and jetpacks.

Cruising Altitude

But maybe things will continue as they have done for the past five years. Cryptocurrencies' actual use stays stable, mostly illegal, largely underground, and completely disconnected from a market price that fluctuates wildly based on the whims of a class of financial speculators with little link to the ground truth. Instability, it turns out, is an oddly stable and predictable state of affairs.

CHAPTER 4

Are Blockchain Technologies Too Complex?

Everything on the Blockchain

Stefaan Verhulst

Stefaan Verhulst is the co-founder and Chief Research and Development Officer of the Governance Laboratory at New York University.

We live in a data age, and it has become common to extol the transformative power of data and information. It is now conventional to assume that many of our most pressing public problems—everything from climate change to terrorism to mass migration—are amenable to a "data fix."

The truth, though, is a little more complicated. While there is no doubt that data—when analyzed and used responsibly—holds tremendous potential, many factors affect whether, and to what extent, that potential will ultimately be fulfilled.

Our ability to address complex public problems using data depends vitally on how our respective data ecosystems is designed (as well as ongoing questions of representation in, power over, and stewardship of these ecosystems).

Flaws in our data ecosystem that prevent us from addressing problems; may also be responsible for many societal failures and inequalities result from the fact that:

- some actors have better access to data than others;
- data is of poor quality (or even "fake"); contains implicit bias; and/or is not validated and thus not trusted;
- only easily accessible data are shared and integrated ("open washing") while important data remain carefully hidden or without resources for relevant research and analysis; and more generally that

"Information Asymmetries, Blockchain Technologies, and Social Change," by Stefaan Verhulst, The Governance Lab, July 24, 2018. http://thegovlab.org/information-asymmetries-blockchain-technologies-and-social-change/. Licensed Under CC BY-SA 4.0 International.

- even in an era of big and open data, information too often remains stove-piped, siloed, and generally difficult to access.

Several observers have pointed to the relationship between these information asymmetries and, for example, corruption, financial exclusion, global pandemics, forced mass migration, human rights abuses, and electoral fraud.

Consider the transaction costs, power inequities and other obstacles that result from such information asymmetries, namely:

- At the individual level: too often someone who is trying to open a bank account (or sign up for new cell phone service) is unable to provide all the requisite information, such as credit history, proof of address or other confirmatory and trusted attributes of identity. As such, information asymmetries are in effect limiting this individual's access to financial and communications services.
- At the corporate level, a vast body of literature in economics has shown how uncertainty over the quality and trustworthiness of data can impose transaction costs, limit the development of markets for goods and services, or shut them down altogether. This is the well-known "market for lemons" problem made famous in a 1970 paper of the same name by George Akerlof.
- At the societal or governance level, information asymmetries don't just affect the efficiency of markets or social inequality. They can also incentivize unwanted behaviors that cause substantial public harm. Tyrants and corrupt politicians thrive on limiting their citizens' access to information (e.g., information related to bank accounts, investment patterns or disbursement of public funds). Likewise, criminals, operate and succeed in the information-scarce corners of the underground economy.

Blockchain Technologies and Information Asymmetries

This is where blockchain comes in. At their core, blockchain technologies are a new type of disclosure mechanism that have the potential to address some of the information asymmetries listed above. There are many types of blockchain technologies, and while I use the blanket term "blockchain" in the below for simplicity's sake, the nuances between different types of blockchain technologies can greatly impact the character and likelihood of success of a given initiative.

By leveraging a shared and verified database of ledgers stored in a distributed manner, blockchain seeks to redesign information ecosystems in a more transparent, immutable, and trusted manner. Solving information asymmetries may be the real potential of blockchain, and this—much more than the current hype over virtual currencies—is the real reason to assess its potential.

It is important to emphasize, of course, that blockchain's potential remains just that for the moment—only *potential*. Considerable hype surrounds the emerging technology, and much remains to be done (and many obstacles overcome) if it is to achieve the enthusiasts' vision of "radical transparency."

At the same time, the following examples and pilots show the various countries and sectors where it is beginning to gain traction—reducing fraud and waste, combating corruption and criminal activity, and generally increasing transparency and reducing information asymmetries.

- Moldova seeks to fight human trafficking by leveraging blockchain to establish an immutable identity for children living in rural areas. For many of these children, a lack of identification documents or other data makes them invisible and untraceable across borders to authorities, and thus makes them vulnerable to exploitation by human traffickers.
- To prevent voter fraud as a result of information asymmetries, Ukraine is using E-vox, which leverages smart contracts in

order to fulfill a number of Ukrainian legal requirements. The system integrates multiple types of identity verification to increase the integrity of the voting system.

- Bext360, a Colorado-based startup, uses smart contracts to pay coffee farmers fairly and on time. It uses a price determined through weighing and analyzing beans by the Bext360 machine, and helps small farmers overcome information asymmetries related to pricing and other market data.
- WeTrust aims to create a more inclusive financial system that would allow anyone to access fair, equitable financial services without an expensive trusted third party.
- BanQu creates an economic passport for previously unbanked populations by using blockchain to record economic and financial transactions and purchase goods. It thus allows unbanked populations to establish and "prove" their identity in global supply chains.

Three Ways Blockchain Technologies Address Information Asymmetries

These and other examples highlight that blockchain technologies can broadly address information asymmetries in three ways:

1. Addressing information asymmetries at the supply and value chain by improving track and trace: The impact of blockchain is already starting to be felt in global supply chains, including in the pharmaceuticals and food industries. By immutably recording various steps in supply chains, (and other logistics chains), blockchain has the potential to reduce waste and fraud, crack down on duplicates and illicit products, and increase consumer safety. Blockchain in effect allows transparency watchdogs, as well as average consumers, to track the provenance of goods they purchase and consume, (such as diamonds), in the process leveraging the power of

information so that consumers and citizens can make better choices.

2. Addressing asymmetries related to the management of identity attributes: The lack of verifiable, self-sovereign identities is emerging as one of the major problems of the information age, enabling everything from identity theft to privacy violations, new and existing forms of surveillance, and other forms of fraud. Today, citizens do not control their online presences, and this not only leads to immediate problems but erodes long-term trust in the entire data ecosystem. Several projects are underway to use blockchain to remedy this situation. For example, the Illinois Blockchain Initiative launched a pilot project testing the value and feasibility of putting citizen birth certificates on the blockchain, giving citizens more control and an easier way to verify their identities. Likewise, Massachusetts Institute of Technology (MIT) is in the second year of a project providing blockchain-based digital diplomas to students. Though still reliant on the registrar's office, the project aims to provide alums with more control over their credentials and the ability of others to view them.

3. Addressing transactional inefficiencies resulting from information asymmetries through smart contracting: Much has been made of blockchain's potential for automated contracting. Smart contracting has the potential to reduce fraud and transaction costs for businesses, governments and citizens. More generally, it has the potential to drastically simplify processes (by, for example, automating compliance and enforcement), thus opening up new business models and permitting average citizens to enter into complex and hitherto expensive arrangements with businesses, governments and each other. Smart contracting is an example of how existing information asymmetries can potentially be leveled and

flattened, putting more power into the hands of citizens and consumers.

Blockchain Technologies and Traditional Means of Addressing Information Asymmetries

To date, information asymmetries needed to be overcome through a variety of institutional and "signalling" means—such as the enforcement of liability and traceability provisions and/or disclosure requirements or monitoring by well-known and trusted institutions; the establishment of industry standards or professional norms; reputation-based mechanisms; or even "outcome-contingent" contracts (where the buyer does not pay until the outcome of the service is known). Recent developments toward "open data" or "open contracting" as part of the move toward "open government" can also be portrayed as efforts to prevent or address information (and power) asymmetries.

These institutional solutions, however, are dependent not just upon strong and trusted societal intermediaries but also upon an individual's ability to access those intermediaries, or leverage the data made available, which explains why information asymmetries affect less developed countries and already excluded people more.

Whether blockchain technologies will provide a distributed, more egalitarian and democratic alternative to these institutional solutions remains to be seen as the presence of these same trust providing mechanisms may in fact be conditional for blockchain to be successfully implemented. Similarly, recent developments toward more private and permission-based blockchains may actually create new or reinforce existing information asymmetries instead of dismantling them (as we have seen with certain identity and smart contracting initiatives—and with ICO token offerings).

To monitor the potential of blockchain for social change—by tackling information asymmetries—The GovLab at NYU, an action-oriented think tank, is compiling a database of blockchain examples from around the world, and welcomes additions sent to blockchange@thegovlab.org.

Blockchain Is a Complex Solution Without a Problem

Greta Bull

Greta Bull is the CEO of the Consultative Group to Assist the Poor and a director at the World Bank.

Countless column inches have been dedicated to distributed ledger technology (DLT) and blockchain since Bitcoin burst onto the global scene in 2009. Since then, numerous financial institutions, governments and other organizations have experimented with testing and implementing blockchain solutions. This includes development organizations such as the World Bank, IMF and the United Nations. Despite breathless enthusiasm and substantial investment, we have seen relatively few DLT applications successfully introduced at scale outside of cryptocurrencies (and these are a whole other can of worms). At CGAP, we have been thinking about which blockchain applications might make sense for financial inclusion, considering use cases such as retail payments, cross-border payments, remittances and agricultural value chains.

The question we have is not "Does blockchain work?" but "Does it work better than other technology solutions in the market?" And what are the cost-benefit trade-offs to switching to a new consensus-based technology solution? We have seen lots of proofs of concept that it can work, but not a lot of quantified analysis on why a DLT solution might be better than existing alternatives.

So, to what extent is blockchain a solution in search of a problem? There are a few important hurdles for those considering blockchain solutions in the financial inclusion space.

"Blockchain: A Solution in Search of a Problem?" by Greta Bull, Consultative Group to Assist the Poor (CGAP), May 29, 2018. http://www.cgap.org/blog/blockchain-solution-search-problem. Licensed under CC BY 3.0.

Governance, Rules, Oversight

The financial services space is highly regulated, and with good reason: There are important restrictions placed on organizations that move money to ensure they are not facilitating criminal or terrorist activities. There are important considerations around financial sector stability, as well as privacy. While blockchain can create an immutable record of two parties agreeing to a transaction, in the financial sector, we must also ensure the information entered into the ledger is legal and compliant with relevant regulations. As such, participants in a financial sector blockchain are likely to be licensed counterparties using a permissioned ledger, either in consortium or with third-party providers who set the rules that others agree to when they join the network. With the exception of a purely private scheme, the complexity of establishing governance arrangements and rules is not much different than that of setting up a payment system today, whether retail or wholesale. In this context, it is unclear that there are significant gains to be made from deploying DLT because the problem is around governance and rules, not technology.

Regulation

In many financial inclusion use cases, the factor slowing things down is not technology, but regulation. Many payment systems, including cross-border systems, operate in real time. What slows things down is regulatory requirements, mainly related to anti-money laundering and combating the financing of terrorism (AML/CFT) or exchange controls. For example, in South Africa, I can send money instantaneously within South Africa using Real Time Clearing, but if I send money into the country, it can take days to get to my account. I recently used PayPal's Xoom service to send money to bank accounts in the United Kingdom and South Africa. The transfer to the United Kingdom took five hours, end to end. Sending money to South Africa took five days (and resulted in my account being frozen for two weeks) because of the South African

Reserve Bank's exchange control policy and required processes. That is not a technology problem: It is a regulatory one. That said, from an operator's perspective, DLT could help reduce the cost of cross-border transfers by making net settlement positions known in real time to all participants, lowering liquidity management costs and minimizing foreign exchange risks. These efficiency gains are great for banks, but it is unclear whether and how these benefits will be passed on to consumers. There is potential here, but we have not yet seen it play out in practice. And it is possible this would be manageable with existing technology solutions.

Privacy, Complexity, Scalability

Privacy is a major and growing challenge in the financial inclusion space. And putting proper privacy controls in place adds complexity to systems that are not centrally managed. SWIFT, the entity that handles cross-border payments on behalf of its member banks, recently completed a well-documented proof of concept using DLT among 28 of its 11,000 member banks. Although SWIFT reported that the test went extremely well, it concluded that further progress is needed on DLT before it can be ready for production-grade applications. It was clear from the test that the clearing of nostro accounts could be streamlined using DLT. But privacy was an issue: Running the test with just 28 banks required 528 subledgers to maintain the confidentiality of information. SWIFT calculated that rolling this out to its entire membership would require the creation of 100,000 subledgers, which would be a challenge to manage. This kind of complexity requires scalability of processing, and this is an area where current database solutions outperform DLT. Using today's technology, Visa can process 24,000 transactions per second. The best I have been able to find that any DLT can do is 1,500-2,000 transactions per second. The sequential nature of DLT and the possibility of forks (incompatible versions) in the ledger because of errors or asynchronous entries introduce additional inefficiencies as solutions scale.

Intersection with Cash Economy

In financial inclusion, which is about bringing the poor into the financial system, there is a major challenge around the way new technologies intersect with the cash economy. No matter how money is sent around the world digitally, poor people need to be able to access and use their financial resources in cash, at least until better solutions are available for paying digitally. Mobile money has garnered a lot of attention in recent years for the important role it has played in improving financial inclusion for the poor. But mobile money is only partly a technology solution. It is mainly a cash distribution business — the cash-in/cash-out interface is critical for enabling people operating in the cash economy to use the system. There are a lot of interesting experiments underway to shift to a more digital profile. For example, using smartphones and QR codes can substantially lower the cost of delivering a payments service. But these solutions rely heavily on people having access to smartphones and bank accounts, which is not yet the case in many poorer parts of the world. And smartphones and QR codes don't need DLT. Mobile network operators, with 2.9 million active cash-in/cash-out agents worldwide, currently reach the poor very effectively, as is clearly validated by the World Bank's Global Findex. And they are increasingly adding use cases like international remittances. GSMA estimates that the cost of sending remittances to Africa can be cut in half by sending remittances via mobile money. But this works on existing technology. It is not evident that DLT makes it work better, particularly in environments where both 3G and electricity access are sketchy.

Recourse

Finally, any DLT solutions would have to incorporate mechanisms related to recourse and consumer protection, whether accepting liability for fraud or helping consumers to find payments that have gone astray or data entries that are incorrect. This is not necessarily the responsibility of the distributed ledger operator, but rules of engagement would need to be agreed to and implemented consistently among system participants. Recourse is critical to building consumer confidence and trust. Liability also enforces good provider practices: Visa and Mastercard have strong fraud management processes in place that limit fraud to a few basis points in a trillion-dollar industry. This is despite the existence of large and sophisticated crime syndicates that are focused on hacking the system.

In the financial inclusion space, we have not yet seen business models emerge that make a compelling case for DLT over existing technology solutions with trusted third-party managers. Ripple is perhaps the one exception to this, but it is basically a managed third-party solution by virtue of its business model, and there is not yet a clear connection to financial inclusion.

That is not to say solutions that incorporate DLT will not emerge. Places where we think there may be breakthroughs are mostly in areas where distributed, real-time information is important: supply chain finance, agricultural value chains, identity verification, personal data storage, clearing and settlement, collateral and land registries and maybe credit reporting. But even these use cases will require answers to some of the questions outlined above. The key point is to understand the trade-offs involved in introducing DLT and to have a clear understanding of the problem you are trying to solve. After creating a proof point to determine whether the technology can work, it then becomes important to conduct a cost-benefit analysis to see if it offers any gains over existing technology solutions. By jumping straight into DLT, you risk putting the solution before the problem.

A Critical Case Study of Blockchain in the Developing World

Thalia Holmes

Thalia Holmes is a South African freelance journalist who has also worked as a writer for the Mail *and the* Guardian.

S imo Mcunu, the VP of Africa at Cashaa Ltd, is exhausted. "I've been working 12 hours a day, seven days a week since our ICO [initial coin offering] went live almost a month ago," he says. "A lot of people want to take advantage of the sale."

Cashaa has ambitious goals. Apart from having already sold more than 100 million tokens of its newly released cryptocurrency called the CAS token, the company aims to use blockchain technology to build "the largest payment platform on earth" as a way to provide peer-to-peer and remittance services at the "cheapest possible rates" to "the next billion"—a reference to the current approximately two billion people who are currently unbanked, according to estimates by Global Findex.

"We are basically a decentralised wallet," says Mcunu. "Traditionally when sending money from overseas to South Africa you would have to wait 72 hours and use three different banks. Now with Cashaa, we are able to do the exact same process but for free and actually instantaneously. It's just one of a few ways that blockchain is changing the world."

Mcunu's flat-out work pace, the "revolutionary" tone of his rhetoric and the hugely ambitious aims of his company capture the zeitgeist of the current cryptocurrency space. Poster child Bitcoin's meteoric rise gives one a sense of this: in 2009, when Bitcoin pioneered the idea of a "virtual," decentralised currency based on a secure, shared digital ledger which cut out the middle

"No Magic Bullet: Cryptocurrencies and Complexities in Africa," by Thalia Holmes, Africa Portal, South African Institute of International Affairs, December 14, 2017. Reprinted by permission.

man and allowed for low-risk, irreversible transactions to take place, bitcoins were worth less than one hundredth of a US cent.

By July 2011, a bitcoin cost $31. By December 2013, one bitcoin would have cost you between $600 and $1000, depending on when you bought it. Fast forward four years to May 2017 and you would have spent $2000 on a bitcoin. In November, it breached the $10,000 mark. A single bitcoin is currently worth over $12,000. Although plagued by huge volatilities, its spectacular rise in price and popularity is almost mythical, made only more so by the fact that its inventor, so-called Satoshi Nakamoto's whereabouts are not known. (According to an October 2017 *Time* magazine article, he could be worth about $5.8-billion).

A veritable explosion of cryptocurrencies, all leveraging blockchain technology, have sprung up in Bitcoin's wake. As of the end of November 2017, there were an estimated 1,324 cryptocurrencies (and counting) available on the internet. Payment platforms, wallets, global settlement networks and hundreds of cryptocurrencies abound. With about 47% marketshare, Bitcoin is still by far the biggest cryptocurrency player but it's being energetically chased by the likes of Ethereum, Litecoin, Ripple and Dash.

What's All the Excitement About?

Bitcoin leverages a technology called blockchain, which is the real crux of the movement. Blockchain is a distributed digital ledger that allows participants to inexpensively and transparently record transactions in a permanent, traceable way.

"One way to think about a blockchain is as a public bulletin board to which anyone can post a transaction record," explained Nir Kshetri, professor of management at the University of North Carolina. "Those posts have to be digitally signed in a particular way, and once posted, a record can never be changed or deleted. The data are stored on many different computers around the internet, and even around the world.

"Together, these features—openness to writing and inspection, authentication through computerised cryptography and redundant storage—provide a mechanism for secure exchange of funds."

As blockchain has matured, it's become apparent that it can be used not only for the exchange of value, but in many other ways as well. Products such as Ethereum have evolved (with about 19% of the total market share, it's the second biggest player). Ethereum is an open software platform based on blockchain technology that enables developers to build and run a wealth of decentralised applications. Potentially, blockchain can be used anywhere the need to track the ownership of documents, assets, or voting rights might exist.

"It can be used in shipping, healthcare, supply chain management, the food industry," explained Mcunu. "The blockchain streamlines all the transactions contained in inbound and outbound logistics: all of that info is no longer going to be stored in a silo but integrated, making it faster and cheaper to use and store."

Solving Real Problems

Several uses are being adapted specifically to Africa. Firstly, blockchain-enabled remittance services are helping people send money to and from Ghana, Zimbabwe, Uganda, Sierra Leone and Rwanda at a fraction of the current banking rates. Along with its advantages, the use of cryptocurrencies for remittances in Africa also has its potential drawbacks.

Chief of Mission for the International Organisation for Migration in South Africa, Richard Ots, said: "Migrants throughout Africa may feel attracted by virtual currencies as a way to remit their earnings to relatives in their country of origin. The cost of regular channels of sending remittances between many countries continues to remain high, and virtual currencies aim to offer an alternative way to save or transmit migrants' earnings. However, the fluctuations in the rates could lead to significant and unexpected decreases in the amounts relatives at home end up saving or receiving".

In Zimbabwe, where assets lost huge amounts of value overnight during the hyperinflation period of 2008, some of its citizens have turned to cryptocurrency as a savings mechanism. According to Verengai Mabika, the founder of BitFinance (now Golix) in Zimbabwe, 37% of Zimababweans use it for this purpose.

When long-time president Robert Mugabe was ousted by the Zimbabwean military in November, Bitcoin saw a surge in price on the Harare exchange. When uncertainty was at its peak, the price for a single bitcoin on the Harare bitcoin exchange was close to double the price on global bitcoin exchanges.

"Interest in bitcoin has peaked as people cannot send money outside or pay for international transactions using formal banks," Yeukai Kusangaya, a trade coordinator at the Golix bitcoin exchange in Zimbabwe, told *Quartz*.

"People have had to look for alternatives and bitcoin has been a useful solution which can be used to purchase goods on Amazon or to pay for vehicles from international suppliers and traders."

Bitcoin has been used to fundraise for projects in Africa since 2013, where a woman in Botswana raised $1,500 for SOS Children's Villages. It can provide a secure voting platform for countries in which citizens might battle to access voting stations or face intimidation.

Blockchain is responsible for movements such as Usizo, a South Africa-based blockchain platform that allows members of the public help pay electricity bills for community schools. And, in a change that will affect every African country with a seaport, blockchain is doing away with the need for paper documents in the tracking of goods by sea, a difficulty that could previously not be met by electronic bills due to the need for non-forgeability and a central register.

There's also its potential to alleviate the circumstances of African refugees. In May, the United Nation's World Food Programme used a blockchain platform to record and authenticate transfers of items such as lentils, pasta and oil for about 10,000 Syrian refugees. The European Union and the United Nations are currently exploring the potential for blockchain to provide legal identification to those who don't have documents. The potential application for this on the African continent is vast.

"Without email, phones, passports or even birth certificates, a blockchain could be the only way many poor people have to prove who they are," says Kshetri. "That could really make their lives better and expand their opportunities."

Adoption in Africa

Thabang Mashiloane, chief executive and co-founder of Chankura Crypto Exchange, a global crypto-currency exchange founded in South Africa and currently headquartered in Silicon Valley, pointed out the rising interest and excitement in certain countries.

"Between August and September 2017, South Africa was the top country in the world to search for the bitcoin term on Google search," Mashiloane told the Africa Portal. "South Africa and Nigeria have seen significant growth in Bitcoin trading from multiple local exchanges. More than $3.6-million is being traded daily in [these] countries. Other African countries such as Kenya, Ghana, and Morocco also have volumes, but due to lack of bitcoin exchanges the volumes are not easily traced."

Gareth Grobler, of cryptocurrency platform ICE3X estimates that between 200,000 and 300,000 South Africans are now involved with cryptocurrencies.

Marina Niforos, principal at Logos Global Advisors which compiled a report about blockchain in emerging markets to the World Bank, described the keen interest of the Kenyan market. "Seventy percent of all transactions in Kenya are already digital and over half percent of the country's adult population holds an M-Pesa digital wallet," she said in a note.

With the most mature mobile money market in Africa, Kenya is leveraging its existing networks to allow for the transactional use of Bitcoin in the country. This is allowing for an easier exchange between fiat and cryptocurrency.

"The lack of an official or formal bitcoin payment gateway has done little to dampen the adoption rate of cryptocurrencies in Kenya. Quite the opposite in fact," said Michael Kimani, chairperson of the Blockchain Association of Kenya. "People have adapted to this service gap by forming peer-to-peer networks where anyone can buy or sell cryptocurrency. These informal networks, resemble the airtime currency informal networks of pre-2006, that powered remittance payment networks before M-Pesa became a thing."

Niforos explained: "With relatively small legacy systems in Africa, the adoption of blockchain becomes easier due to lower transition costs and less cultural resistance. This provides the backdrop for ... disruption in the remittances and payments segment.

"Peer-to-peer payments with digital currencies have started to become an alternative to local currencies, with a number of growing blockchain African-run startups, including Kenya's BitPesa and Bitsoko, Ghana's bitcoin exchanges BTCGhana, and South Africa's Luno and Ice3X and GeoPay, BitSure and Chankura. South African mobile money network PayFast recently integrated bitcoin payments options and now provides access for bitcoin payment to 30,000 merchants outlets across the country."

Where Could This All Be Leading?

The higher risks associated with traditional banking, lower bank penetration, and greater presence of digital financing in most African markets provide fertile ground for a "technological leap forward and a boost to financial inclusion and growth," said Niforos.

Bashir Aminu, the founder of Cryptogene, a Nigerian-based multi-platform hub for the development of blockchain technology, said that he sees the potential for blockhain "more in Africa than anywhere else."

"Blockchain technology presents us with an opportunity to solve the problem of financial inclusion, [among] other things," he told the *Africa Portal*. "In other parts of the world where they have legacy systems, they don't need this as much as we do."

Philip Asare, the chief executive officer of bitcoin exchange BtcGhana, believes that cryptocurrencies can usher in a new era of prosperity to Africa. "Ultimately, blockchain technology will help in bringing wealth to a land plagued by poverty," he said. "A decentralised system like Bitcoin will spur interconnected hubs of prosperity that function beyond national boundaries."

What Are the Challenges?

While these advancements would be welcome in Africa, the implementation of a solution that requires a high level of technological know-how, financial literacy, access to internet and a computer or smartphone has its challenges. The World Bank's 2014 Global Financial Index found that 66% of Sub-Saharan Africans did not have a bank account, and only 20% of Africans own a smartphone, according to a 2015 report by Pew Research Centre.

In Aminu's experience with Cryptogene in Nigeria, there's a huge need for consumer education around the benefits of cryptocurrency and blockchain applications. "Our biggest challenge is getting people to understand the use cases of this technology—that it can actually help them," said Aminu. For that reason, "education is the first part in our roadmap," he continued. "People will most likely not adopt what they don't understand."

Cryptogene holds regular webinars, lectures and group training sessions for its members. Since its inception about a year ago, the Cryptogene community has grown to about 5000 people from Nigeria and surrounds, ranging from tech experts to people who know very little about cryptocurrencies. To address a generally low level of financial literacy, its founders aim to eventually develop a user-friendly, accessible platform for remittances.

"When you are using it, you don't need to know that it's blockchain you are using," said Aminu. "Of course, behind the scenes is the whole blockchain thing, but we want to make it feel like a traditional system."

Internet access is another prohibitive factor. "The cost of internet connection has improved significantly over the past couple of years, but it's still not accessible to the vast majority of the population," said Aminu, with the experience of Africa's largest economy being reflective of most others.

Thomas Rehermann, an economist for the International Finance Corporation who specialises in the cryptocurrency space, points out the added concern of electricity costs. "One of the biggest challenges is the lack of access to cheap electricity," he told the *Africa Portal*. "Electricity in most African countries is much more expensive than in countries with similar or somewhat higher income. Therefore, the triangle of banks / nonbank fintechs, telecommunication companies and energy / electricity providers must be integrated much better in yet-to-be-accessed places."

And, in order to use cryptocurrencies, Africans need to be able to exchange their fiat currency into the desired crypto. This requires an exchange or wallet, and there's a dearth of these in many countries around the continent. "The challenge in majority of the African countries has been the lack of bitcoin infrastructure companies like exchanges that allow users to exchange between fiat and bitcoin," said Mashiloane. "There's only a few African countries with fiat to cryptocurrency exchanges."

Langelihle Mnyandu, an associate in the Banking and Finance department at Bowmans Law Firm, pointed out that money in Africa is still very much paper-based. "One misconception about money in Africa is that it is digital. It's not. It's still in hard paper," he said in an interview with *Africa Portal*.

"If you have a funder in the US looking to sponsor a project involving rural people in Africa who have little access to technology, how do you get those funds to them using blockchain?" he said. "At the end of the day, you're going to have to convert that cash to a fiat currency, which is cash that the people can use." In Mnyandu's opinion, it will "be very difficult to totally remove banks, because they are still a big part of this ecosystem".

Regulation

And speaking of banks, cryptocurrencies' traditional financial counterparts conform to endless standards and regulation. How is Africa regulating this new type of transaction, which by nature is decentralised and can be conducted anonymously?

A "standout challenge" in this regard "is the matter of jurisdiction," said Mnyandu. "Blockchain and cryptocurrencies are cloud-based products and services, so now the biggest issues facing regulators is whether they have the appropriate jurisdiction to pass laws and regulate," he said. "At what point do you determine and say this is a 'South African' blockchain?"

The only way to address this, he said, is by collaboration between governments and sectors. Regulators across Africa need to work together to come up with solutions that transcend borders.

There's also a need to "regulate efficiently," said Mnyandu. "This space is forever changing, so before you come out and pass regulations, it's very important to understand what this revolution is all about and where the trends are going – so that when you pass the regulations you don't stifle the innovation side of it."

Bright Tibane, a senior associate in the same department at Bowmans Law Firm, said that one way of doing this was by adopting an approach called sandboxing. This practice creates a regulatory framework that forms the space for innovators to break the rules, and then allows them to demonstrate that breaking the rules has not been detrimental in that particular case. The United Kingdom and Singapore are following this approach. South African authorities are looking to adopt something similar. "It's a way of ensuring what's going on, testing innovations in a safe space, and then that enables you to regulate efficiently," said Tibane.

In addition to South Africa, Uganda has shown proactivity in its approach to regulation, says Tibane. "These are not things they're just sitting on—they are actually looking at substantive cases as to how to they can regulate this thing," said Tibane.

And generally, African regulators have been fairly receptive to cryptocurrencies, they said. "There is no African jurisdiction which has come out to say they don't like the model or totally prohibit it," said Tibane.

Could Cryptocurrencies Really Lead to a Financial Revolution in Africa?

While many blockchain evangelists offer an unreserved yes in answer to this question, others are more tempered in their views.

According to Moashilane, cryptocurrencies will offer revolution in established markets, and a different kind of change in Africa. "I believe cryptocurrencies are going to change the way the world operates from central banking to decentralised blockchain applications that disrupt Silicon Valley and Wall Street," said Moashilane. But, "in most African countries there hasn't been major global financial institutions to disrupt, so cryptocurrencies provide another opportunity to skip telephones for mobile phones."

In Mcunu's opinion, blockchain will underscore a mighty shift in the way we transact, but he cautions that the hype has created a price bubble around some of the tokens. "Once the bubble is over, we will see the real intrinsic value of the tokens, and those are the ones that actually have utility," he said.

Rehermann highlights an argument made in the *Harvard Business Review* that "much of the most imminent benefits from blockchain (and by extension cryptocurrencies) are incremental and rather hidden from customers (for example, internal reconciliation of accounts and settlements)".

"The truly transformational changes might come rather later in technical terms," he said. "However, the sheer number of unbanked people in Africa might mean that even incremental, low-key offerings go a long way to simply include populations not yet participating at all in transactions."

In the meantime, cryptocurrencies and their protagonists continue to think and act big. Once the Cashaa ICO ends in December, "then we are going to start working on our main project," said Mcunu. "We will launch our multicurrency wallet in India, the UK, Africa, the Philippines and Asia. Eventually, we'll open a lending unit and an insurance unit. You might think I'm sounding like a salesperson here, but this stuff is really, really good."

Bitcoin Mining Is an Environmental Hazard

Christopher Malmo

Christopher Malmo is a writer for Vice Media's Motherboard *vertical.*

As Bitcoin's price increases, its energy consumption is soaring. Bitcoin's power consumption is extremely high compared to conventional digital payment, and one transaction now uses as much energy as your house in a week.

Bitcoin's incredible price run to break over $7,000 this year has sent its overall energy consumption soaring, as people worldwide bring more energy-hungry computers online to mine the digital currency.

Bitcoin mining is the largely automated process (although it can be done by hand) of finding a particular hash value that "solves" a block of transaction data, adding it to an ever-growing chain of blocks that is referred to, appropriately, as the blockchain. Mining secures this distributed ledger of transactions, but it isn't cheap: The most successful miners operate warehouses full of specialized machines constantly crunching numbers. Solving a block releases some new bitcoins to the miner as a reward for their work, making it a potentially lucrative venture, but what's the environmental cost?

How Much Energy Does Bitcoin Mining Consume?

An index from cryptocurrency analyst Alex de Vries, aka Digiconomist, estimates that with prices the way they are now, it would be profitable for Bitcoin miners to burn through over 24 terawatt-hours of electricity annually as they compete to solve increasingly difficult cryptographic puzzles to "mine" more Bitcoins. That's about as much as Nigeria, a country of 186 million people, uses in a year.

"One Bitcoin Transaction Consumes As Much Energy As Your House Uses in a Week," by Christopher Malmo, Motherboard, Vice Media, November 1, 2017. Reprinted by permission.

This averages out to a shocking 215 kilowatt-hours (KWh) of juice used by miners for each Bitcoin transaction (there are currently about 300,000 transactions per day). Since the average American household consumes 901 KWh per month, each Bitcoin transfer represents enough energy to run a comfortable house, and everything in it, for nearly a week. On a larger scale, De Vries' index shows that bitcoin miners worldwide could be using enough electricity to at any given time to power about 2.26 million American homes.

Expressing Bitcoin's energy consumption on a per-transaction basis is a useful abstraction. Bitcoin uses x energy in total, and this energy verifies/secures roughly 300k transactions per day. So this measure shows the value we get for all that electricity, since the verified transaction (and our confidence in it) is ultimately the end product.

What Is Bitcoin's Environmental Impact?

It's worth asking ourselves hard questions about Bitcoin's environmental impact.

Since 2015, Bitcoin's electricity consumption has been very high compared to conventional digital payment methods. This is because the dollar price of Bitcoin is directly proportional to the amount of electricity that can profitably be used to mine it. As the price rises, miners add more computing power to chase new Bitcoins and transaction fees.

It's impossible to know *exactly* how much electricity the Bitcoin network uses. But we can run a quick calculation of the *minimum* energy Bitcoin could be using, assuming that all miners are running the most efficient hardware with no efficiency losses due to waste heat. To do this, we'll use a simple methodology laid out in previous coverage on Motherboard. This would give us a constant total mining draw of just over one gigawatt.

That means that, at a minimum, worldwide Bitcoin mining could power the daily needs of 821,940 average American homes.

Put another way, global Bitcoin mining represents a minimum of 77KWh of energy consumed *per Bitcoin transaction.* Even as an unrealistic lower boundary, this figure is high: As senior economist Teunis Brosens from Dutch bank ING wrote, it's enough to power his own home in the Netherlands for nearly two weeks.

Digiconomist's less optimistic estimate for per-transaction energy costs now sits at around 215 KWh of electricity. That's more than enough to fill two Tesla batteries, run an efficient fridge/freezer for a full year, or boil 1872 litres of water in a kettle.

It's important to remember that de Vries' model isn't exact. It makes assumptions about the economic incentives available to miners at a given price level, and presents a forward-looking prediction for where mining electricity consumption *could* go. Despite this, it's quite clear that even at the minimum level of 77 KWh per transaction, we have a problem. At 215 KWh, we have an even bigger problem.

That problem is carbon emissions. De Vries has come up with some estimates by diving into data made available on a coal-powered Bitcoin mine in Mongolia. He concluded that this single mine is responsible for 8,000 to 13,000 kg CO_2 emissions per Bitcoin it mines, and 24,000 - 40,000 kg of CO_2 per hour.

As Twitter user Matthias Bartosik noted in some similar estimates, the average European car emits 0.1181 kg of CO_2 per kilometer driven. So for every hour the Mongolian Bitcoin mine operates, it's responsible for (at least) the CO_2 equivalent of over 203,000 car kilometers travelled.

Can Bitcoin Reduce Its Massive Energy Consumption?

As goes the Bitcoin price, so goes its electricity consumption, and therefore its overall carbon emissions. I asked de Vries whether it was possible for Bitcoin to scale its way out of this problem.

"Blockchain is inefficient tech by design, as we create trust by building a system based on distrust. If you only trust yourself and a set of rules (the software), then you have to validate everything that happens against these rules yourself. That is the life of a blockchain node," he said via direct message.

This gets to the heart of Bitcoin's core innovation, and also its core compromise. In order to achieve a functional, trustworthy decentralized payment system, Bitcoin imposes some very costly inefficiencies on participants, for example voracious electricity consumption and low transaction capacity. Proposed improvements, like SegWit2x, do promise to increase the number of transactions Bitcoin can handle by at least double, and decrease network congestion. But since Bitcoin is thousands of times less efficient per transaction than a credit card network, it will need to get thousands of times better.

In the context of climate change, raging wildfires, and record-breaking hurricanes, it's worth asking ourselves hard questions about Bitcoin's environmental impact, and what we want to use it for. Do most transactions actually need to bypass trusted third parties like banks and credit card companies, which can operate much more efficiently than Bitcoin's decentralized network? Imperfect as these financial institutions are, for most of us, the answer is very likely no.

The Blockchain Is Just a Ledger

Michael J. Casey and Paul Vigna

Michael Casey is a senior lecturer on global economics and management at MIT. Paul Vigna is a reporter for the Wall Street Journal. *Both are authors of* The Age of Cryptocurrency: How Bitcoin and Digital Money Are Challenging the Global Economic Order.

The dot-com bubble of the 1990s is popularly viewed as a period of crazy excess that ended with hundreds of billions of dollars of wealth being destroyed. What's less often discussed is how all the cheap capital of the boom years helped fund the infrastructure upon which the most important internet innovations would be built after the bubble burst. It paid for the rollout of fiber-optic cable, R&D in 3G networks, and the buildout of giant server farms. All of this would make possible the technologies that are now the bedrock of the world's most powerful companies: algorithmic search, social media, mobile computing, cloud services, big-data analytics, AI, and more.

We think something similar is happening behind the wild volatility and stratospheric hype of the cryptocurrency and blockchain boom. The blockchain skeptics have crowed gleefully as crypto-token prices have tumbled from last year's dizzying highs, but they make the same mistake as the crypto fanboys they mock: they conflate price with inherent value. We can't yet predict what the blue-chip industries built on blockchain technology will be, but we are confident that they will exist, because the technology itself is all about creating one priceless asset: trust.

To understand why, we need to go back to the 14th century.

That was when Italian merchants and bankers began using the double-entry bookkeeping method. This method, made possible by

"In Blockchain We Trust," by Michael J. Casey and Paul Vigna, MIT Technology Review, April 9, 2018. Reprinted by permission.

the adoption of Arabic numerals, gave merchants a more reliable record-keeping tool, and it let bankers assume a powerful new role as middlemen in the international payments system. Yet it wasn't just the tool itself that made way for modern finance. It was how it was inserted into the culture of the day.

In 1494 Luca Pacioli, a Franciscan friar and mathematician, codified their practices by publishing a manual on math and accounting that presented double-entry bookkeeping not only as a way to track accounts but as a moral obligation. The way Pacioli described it, for everything of value that merchants or bankers took in, they had to give something back. Hence the use of offsetting entries to record separate, balancing values—a debit matched with a credit, an asset with a liability.

Pacioli's morally upright accounting bestowed a form of religious benediction on these previously disparaged professions. Over the next several centuries, clean books came to be regarded as a sign of honesty and piety, clearing bankers to become payment intermediaries and speeding up the circulation of money. That funded the Renaissance and paved the way for the capitalist explosion that would change the world.

Yet the system was not impervious to fraud. Bankers and other financial actors often breached their moral duty to keep honest books, and they still do—just ask Bernie Madoff's clients or Enron's shareholders. Moreover, even when they are honest, their honesty comes at a price. We've allowed centralized trust managers such as banks, stock exchanges, and other financial middlemen to become indispensable, and this has turned them from intermediaries into gatekeepers. They charge fees and restrict access, creating friction, curtailing innovation, and strengthening their market dominance.

The real promise of blockchain technology, then, is not that it could make you a billionaire overnight or give you a way to shield your financial activities from nosy governments. It's that it could drastically reduce the cost of trust by means of a radical, decentralized approach to accounting—and, by extension, create a new way to structure economic organizations.

A new form of bookkeeping might seem like a dull accomplishment. Yet for thousands of years, going back to Hammurabi's Babylon, ledgers have been the bedrock of civilization. That's because the exchanges of value on which society is founded require us to trust each other's claims about what we own, what we're owed, and what we owe. To achieve that trust, we need a common system for keeping track of our transactions, a system that gives definition and order to society itself. How else would we know that Jeff Bezos is the world's richest human being, that the GDP of Argentina is $620 billion, that 71 percent of the world's population lives on less than $10 a day, or that Apple's shares are trading at a particular multiple of the company's earnings per share?

A blockchain (though the term is bandied about loosely, and often misapplied to things that are not really blockchains) is an electronic ledger—a list of transactions. Those transactions can in principle represent almost anything. They could be actual exchanges of money, as they are on the blockchains that underlie cryptocurrencies like Bitcoin. They could mark exchanges of other assets, such as digital stock certificates. They could represent instructions, such as orders to buy or sell a stock. They could include so-called smart contracts, which are computerized instructions to do something (e.g., buy a stock) if something else is true (the price of the stock has dropped below $10).

What makes a blockchain a special kind of ledger is that instead of being managed by a single *centralized* institution, such as a bank or government agency, it is stored in multiple copies on multiple independent computers within a *decentralized* network. No single entity controls the ledger. Any of the computers on the network can make a change to the ledger, but only by following rules dictated by a "consensus protocol," a mathematical algorithm that requires a majority of the other computers on the network to agree with the change.

Once a consensus generated by that algorithm has been achieved, all the computers on the network update their copies of the ledger simultaneously. If any of them tries to add an entry to the ledger without this consensus, or to change an entry retroactively, the rest of the network automatically rejects the entry as invalid.

Typically, transactions are bundled together into blocks of a certain size that are chained together (hence "blockchain") by cryptographic locks, themselves a product of the consensus algorithm. This produces an *immutable,* shared record of the "truth," one that—if things have been set up right—cannot be tampered with.

Within this general framework are many variations. There are different kinds of consensus protocols, for example, and often disagreements over which kind is most secure. There are public, "permissionless" blockchain ledgers, to which in principle anyone can hitch a computer and become part of the network; these are what Bitcoin and most other cryptocurrencies belong to. There are also private, "permissioned" ledger systems that incorporate no digital currency. These might be used by a group of organizations that need a common record-keeping system but are independent of one another and perhaps don't entirely trust one another—a manufacturer and its suppliers, for example.

The common thread between all of them is that mathematical rules and impregnable cryptography, rather than trust in fallible humans or institutions, are what guarantee the integrity of the ledger. It's a version of what the cryptographer Ian Grigg described as "triple-entry bookkeeping": one entry on the debit side, another for the credit, and a third into an immutable, undisputed, shared ledger.

The benefits of this decentralized model emerge when weighed against the current economic system's cost of trust. Consider this: In 2007, Lehman Brothers reported record profits and revenue, all endorsed by its auditor, Ernst & Young. Nine months later, a nosedive in those same assets rendered the 158-year-old business bankrupt, triggering the biggest financial crisis in 80 years. Clearly, the valuations cited in the preceding years' books were way off. And we later learned that Lehman's ledger wasn't the only one with dubious data. Banks in the US and Europe paid out hundreds of billions of dollars in fines and settlements to cover losses caused by inflated balance sheets. It was a powerful reminder of the high price we often pay for trusting centralized entities' internally devised numbers.

The crisis was an extreme example of the cost of trust. But we also find that cost ingrained in most other areas of the economy. Think of all the accountants whose cubicles fill the skyscrapers of the world. Their jobs, reconciling their company's ledgers with those of its business counterparts, exist because neither party *trusts* the other's record. It is a time-consuming, expensive, yet necessary process.

Other manifestations of the cost of trust are felt not in what we do but in what we can't do. Two billion people are denied bank accounts, which locks them out of the global economy because banks don't trust the records of their assets and identities. Meanwhile, the internet of things, which it's hoped will have billions of interacting autonomous devices forging new efficiencies, won't be possible if gadget-to-gadget microtransactions require the prohibitively expensive intermediation of centrally controlled ledgers. There are many other examples of how this problem limits innovation.

These costs are rarely acknowledged or analyzed by the economics profession, perhaps because practices such as account reconciliation are assumed to be an integral, unavoidable feature of business (much as pre-internet businesses assumed they had no option but to pay large postal expenses to mail out monthly bills). Might this blind spot explain why some prominent economists are quick to dismiss blockchain technology? Many say they can't see the justification for its costs. Yet their analyses typically don't weigh those costs against the far-reaching societal cost of trust that the new models seek to overcome.

More and more people get it, however. Since Bitcoin's low-key release in January 2009, the ranks of its advocates have swelled from libertarian-minded radicals to include former Wall Street professionals, Silicon Valley tech mavens, and development and aid experts from bodies such as the World Bank. Many see the technology's rise as a vital new phase in the internet economy—one that is, arguably, even more transformative than the first. Whereas the first wave of online disruption saw brick-and-mortar businesses displaced by leaner digital intermediaries, this movement challenges the whole idea of for-profit middlemen altogether.

The need for trust, the cost of it, and the dependence on middlemen to provide it is one reason why behemoths such as Google, Facebook, and Amazon turn economies of scale and network-effect advantages into de facto monopolies. These giants are, in effect, centralized ledger keepers, building vast records of "transactions" in what is, arguably, the most important "currency" in the world: our digital data. In controlling those records, they control us.

The potential promise of overturning this entrenched, centralized system is an important factor behind the gold-rush-like scene in the crypto-token market, with its soaring yet volatile prices. No doubt many—perhaps most—investors are merely hoping to get rich quick and give little thought to why the technology matters. But manias like this, as irrational as they become, don't spring out of nowhere. As with the arrival of past transformative platform technologies—railroads, for example, or electricity—rampant speculation is almost inevitable. That's because when a big new idea comes along, investors have no framework for estimating how much value it will create or destroy, or for deciding which enterprises will win or lose.

Although there are still major obstacles to overcome before blockchains can fulfill the promise of a more robust system for recording and storing objective truth, these concepts are already being tested in the field.

Companies such as IBM and Foxconn are exploiting the idea of immutability in projects that seek to unlock trade finance and make supply chains more transparent. Such transparency could also give consumers better information on the sources of what they buy—whether a T-shirt was made with sweatshop labor, for example.

Another important new idea is that of a *digital asset.* Before Bitcoin, nobody could own an asset in the digital realm. Since copying digital content is easy to do and difficult to stop, providers of digital products such as MP3 audio files or e-books never give customers outright ownership of the content, but instead lease it and define what users can do with it in a license, with stiff legal penalties if the license is broken. This is why you can make a 14-day loan of your Amazon Kindle book to a friend, but you can't sell it or give it as a gift, as you might a paper book.

Bitcoin showed that an item of value could be both digital and verifiably unique. Since nobody can alter the ledger and "double-spend," or duplicate, a bitcoin, it can be conceived of as a unique "thing" or asset. That means we can now represent any form of value—a property title or a music track, for example—as an entry in a blockchain transaction. And by digitizing different forms of value in this way, we can introduce software for managing the economy that operates around them.

As software-based items, these new digital assets can be given certain "If X, then Y" properties. In other words, money can become *programmable.* For example, you could pay to hire an electric vehicle using digital tokens that also serve to activate or disable its engine, thus fulfilling the encoded terms of a smart contract. It's quite different from analog tokens such as banknotes or metal coins, which are agnostic about what they're used for.

What makes these programmable money contracts "smart" is not that they're automated; we already have that when our bank follows our programmed instructions to autopay our credit card bill every month. It's that the computers executing the contract are monitored by a decentralized blockchain network. That assures all signatories to a smart contract that it will be carried out fairly.

With this technology, the computers of a shipper and an exporter, for example, could automate a transfer of ownership of goods once the decentralized software they both use sends a signal that a digital-currency payment—or a cryptographically unbreakable commitment to pay—has been made. Neither party necessarily trusts the other, but they can nonetheless carry out that automatic transfer without relying on a third party. In this way, smart contracts take automation to a new level—enabling a much more open, global set of relationships.

Programmable money and smart contracts constitute a powerful way for communities to govern themselves in pursuit of common objectives. They even offer a potential breakthrough in the "Tragedy of the Commons," the long-held notion that people can't simultaneously serve their self-interest and the common good. That was evident in many of the blockchain proposals from the 100 software engineers who took part in Hack4Climate at last year's UN climate-change conference in Bonn. The winning team, with a project called GainForest, is now developing a blockchain-based system by which donors can reward communities living in vulnerable rain forests for provable actions they take to restore the environment.

Still, this utopian, frictionless "token economy" is far from reality. Regulators in China, South Korea, and the US have cracked down on issuers and traders of tokens, viewing such currencies more as speculative get-rich-quick schemes that avoid securities laws than as world—changing new economic models. They're not entirely wrong: some developers have pre-sold tokens in "initial coin offerings," or ICOs, but haven't used the money to build and market products. Public or "permissionless" blockchains like Bitcoin and Ethereum, which hold the greatest promise of absolute openness and immutability, are facing growing pains. Bitcoin still can't process more than seven transactions a second, and transaction fees can sometimes spike, making it costly to use.

Meanwhile, the centralized institutions that should be vulnerable to disruption, such as banks, are digging in. They are protected by existing regulations, which are ostensibly imposed to keep them honest but inadvertently constitute a compliance cost for startups. Those regulations, such as the burdensome reporting and capital requirements that the New York State Department of Financial Services' "BitLicense" imposed on cryptocurrency remittance startups, become barriers to entry that protect incumbents.

But here's the thing: the open-source nature of blockchain technology, the excitement it has generated, and the rising value of the underlying tokens have encouraged a global pool of intelligent, impassioned, and financially motivated computer scientists to work on overcoming these limitations. It's reasonable to assume they will constantly improve the tech. Just as we've seen with internet software, open, extensible protocols such as these can become powerful platforms for innovation. Blockchain technology is moving way too fast for us to think later versions won't improve upon the present, whether it's in Bitcoin's cryptocurrency-based protocol, Ethereum's smart-contract-focused blockchain, or some as-yet-undiscovered platform.

The crypto bubble, like the dot-com bubble, is creating the infrastructure that will enable the technologies of the future to be built. But there's also a key difference. This time, the money being raised isn't underwriting *physical* infrastructure but *social* infrastructure. It's creating incentives to form global networks of collaborating developers, hive minds whose supply of interacting, iterative ideas is codified into lines of open-source software. That freely accessible code will enable the execution of countless as-yet-unimagined ideas. It is the foundation upon which the decentralized economy of the future will be built.

Just as few people in the mid-1990s could predict the later emergence of Google, Facebook, and Uber, we can't predict what blockchain-based applications will emerge from the wreckage of this bubble to dominate the decentralized future. But that's what you get with extensible platforms. Whether it's the open protocols of the internet or the blockchain's core components of algorithmic consensus and distributed record-keeping, their power lies in providing an entirely new paradigm for innovators ready to dream up and deploy world-changing applications. In this case, those applications—whatever shape they take—will be aimed squarely at disrupting many of the gatekeeping institutions that currently dominate our centralized economy.

Voting on the Blockchain

Benjamin Freed

Benjamin Freed is the technology editor at StateScoop.

Two months after West Virginia allowed a small group of overseas voters to participate in the May 8 primary election using online ballots powered by blockchain technology, one of the state's top election's officials said on Sunday it could be implemented statewide in time for the general election in November.

If the results of a post-election audit are favorable toward the new technology, which was offered to voters from two counties during the primary, West Virginia will offer all 55 of its counties to participate in blockchain-powered voting, Donald "Deak" Kersey, the state's elections director, said at the National Association of Secretaries of State conference in Philadelphia.

"We have to wait on the audit," Kersey said. But if officials get "something that comes back from someone who knows what they're talking about and says it's secure," Kersey said hundreds more voters may have the option to vote using a mobile app instead of sending a paper ballot through international mail.

West Virginia got two of its counties to participate in the primary experiment after being approached by Tusk Montgomery Philanthropies, a New York venture-capital firm with investments in cryptocurrency exchanges and other companies developing distributed ledger platforms. The state had been looking to modernize the way it gets ballots to its registered voters who live abroad, especially military personnel on deployment, but found most electronic-balloting systems too expensive.

Tusk Montgomery agreed to pay for West Virginia to test out a mobile voting app developed by four-year-old Massachusetts firm Voatz. Kersey said his office recruited the elections chiefs in Monongalia and Harrison counties—which have a combined population of about 143,000—to offer the app to their registered voters not currently residing in the country, including Secretary of State (and Kersey's boss) Mac Warner's son, who is an active-duty Army officer.

West Virginia officials have been coy about how many people actually used Voatz's app during the primary, though a source with knowledge of the project said it was as few as 13. But Kersey sounded confident in the limited sample.

"The factors were it had to be secure, affordable, transparent, auditable and no mail, printer, fax or scanner needed," he said. "The sailor in the submarine under the polar ice cap doesn't have access to US Mail, but he does have access to the internet."

Several Steps for Authentication

With voters and election officials rattled by discoveries of foreign hackers' attempts to meddle in the 2016 presidential election, digital voting systems can face a high level of distrust. But both Kersey and Voatz co-founder Nimit Sawhney defended the company's platform as being highly secure.

A demonstration provided by Sawhney showed that the app goes through several authentication steps, beginning with a six-digit code that's texted to a user's phone and has to be entered back into the app. From there, a user is required to upload an image of a government-issued photo and then take a selfie for verification, which takes up to 24 hours, Sawhney said. Once that is complete, a registered user is finally presented with a ballot.

Critics of new voting technologies frequently cite paper-based ballots as the preferred method to ensure trustworthy election results, and are wary of new technologies like blockchain, which is barely a decade old.

"I know as an elections administrator, it raises a lot of red flags," Kersey said. "But this posed the best options."

Kersey vouched for Voatz by telling a roomful of secretaries of state and other election officials that Warner and his chief information officer, Dave Tackett, personally toured Voatz's office outside Boston and examined the company's computing standards, which it says are set by the National Institute for Standards and Technology and the MITRE Corporation, among other organizations.

Retrieving the actual votes from the app once they've been cast is also a bit elaborate. Kersey said Voatz delivered physical security keys—essentially flash drives with de-encryption codes—to the counties that participated in the pilot, with two users of opposite political parties needed to unlock the votes from the company's server.

"They literally flew from Boston to West Virginia and drove from Morgantown and delivered them to the county clerks," Kersey said. "The reports are printed and votes are cast. Voters are secret."

Kersey said that's an upgrade over other electronic methods overseas voters use to return their ballots. Many Americans voting from abroad who send in their ballots via fax or email are required to sign waivers acknowledging they're giving up the secrecy of their votes.

Within the next week, Kersey said, his office will decide if it wants to roll out Voatz's system across the state, though if it does, it will be on a voluntary basis for every county.

"Oh, My God."

Not everyone who watched Kersey's presentation was convinced that mobile voting is the way to go.

"Oh, my god," said J. Alex Halderman, a computer science professor at the University of Michigan who is serving as a technology fellow to Verified Voting, which advocates for ballot security. "Voting over the internet creates extra-difficult problems. Securing servers? Protecting devices? Assuring votes have been recorded while protecting the secret ballot?"

Halderman said that no voting technology developed is as secure as in-person paper ballots. He's testified before Congress on the subject, and has conducted demonstrations in which he hacked electronic voting machines to change tabulations and, in one case, reprogram a machine to play Pac-Man.

In a recent video he made with the *New York Times* , Halderman explained how a committed hacker—whether acting alone or on behalf of a foreign government—might pose as an election-equipment manufacturer and email a local election official with a virus masked as a software update.

Voatz, Halderman said, "hasn't made enough public about how the tech works for outside experts to scrutinize it."

Sawhney told StateScoop that ballots collected over Voatz can generate paper receipts. He also said that the company's app will not run if it detects malware on a mobile device, but Halderman was skeptical of that claim. "That sounds like a $1 billion solution," he said.

Still, Halderman agreed making it easier for US citizens to vote from abroad, especially deployed military, is a worthy goal.

"We should do everything we can to make sure members of the military can vote," he said. "The biggest thing jurisdictions could do for military voters is to extend their deadlines." (He also expressed doubt that sailors would be allowed to bring their personal mobile phones aboard a submarine.)

If It Works for the Oscars…

But whether it's through blockchain or another protocol, internet and mobile voting is inevitable, and for more than just overseas voters said James Simmons, the chief executive of Everyone Counts, which makes software for voter registration and digital elections, including some overseas ballots.

Most elections Simmons's company conducts are for non-government entities, including corporate boards, labor union leadership and awards shows like the Oscars. He said votes are encrypted with private and public keys and transmitted using secure sockets layer and transport layer security protocols back to independent auditors, who tally the actual votes. (The incident at the 2017 Academy Awards in which *La La Land* was mistakenly named Best Picture over the actual winner, *Moonlight*, was the result of an on-stage misreading, though Simmons said he was momentarily worried that his company's system had failed.)

Simmons did not endorse blockchain or any other specific platform, but he did predict that online voting will spread to the general public.

"One day the world will vote online," he said. "The technology's not there yet. It might be a long way off. But like so much else, it will be digitized."

Even if the the audit of West Virginia's two-county pilot is positive toward Voatz's software, West Virginia does not have a particularly large overseas diaspora—the Federal Voting Assistance Program, which facilitates voting from abroad, counted 334 registered voters from the state living in foreign countries in a 2016 survey. Kersey said he expects to hear the results later this month, just before a meeting with election directors in all 55 counties.

Organizations to Contact

The editors have compiled the following list of organizations concerned with the issues debated in this book. The descriptions are derived from materials provided by the organizations. All have publications or information available for interested readers. This list was compiled on the date of publication of the present volume; the information provided here may change. Be aware that many organizations take several weeks or longer to respond to inquiries, so allow as much time as possible.

Bitcoin Center NYC
157 Prince Street
New York, NY 10012
phone: (917) 515-5355
email: info@bitcoincenternyc.com
website: www.bitcoincenternyc.com

The Bitcoin Center NYC is an organization originally built near the New York Stock Exchange with the intention of coordinating in-person bitcoin trades. The Center also hosts classes and talks on the use of bitcoin and other cryptocurrencies on the blockchain.

BitGive Foundation
PO Box 1697
Truckee, CA 96160
phone: (916) 625-6BIT
email: info@bitgivefoundation.org
website: www.bitgivefoundation.org

The BitGive Foundation was the first bitcoin 501(c)(3) nonprofit. It works to leverage bitcoin and blockchain technologies to benefit charitable organizations worldwide.

Blockchain Academy

The Bandwidth Barn Block B, 3rd Floor
Woodstock Exchange 66-68 Albert Road
Woodstock, Cape Town, 7925
South Africa
phone: 27 (21) 409 7000
email: info@blockchainacademy.co.za
website: www.blockchainacademy.co.za

The Blockchain Academy is a place where entrepreneurs, developers, and institutions from many different industries train to learn about the potential of blockchain technology and cryptocurrencies such as bitcoin. Their website features a number of courses on the subject that can be taken in person and digitally.

Blockchain Alliance

email: jweinstein@steptoe.com
website: www.blockchainalliance.org

The Blockchain Alliance is a public-private forum created by the blockchain community that aims to combat the use of blockchain for illegal activity, along with making the blockchain ecosystem more secure and promoting its use. It does this by serving as an open resource for law enforcement and regulatory agencies as well as by providing education, technical assistance, and periodic informational sessions to the wider public.

Blockchain at Berkeley

email: education@blockchain.berkeley.edu
website: www.blockchain.berkeley.edu

Blockchain at Berkeley is a student-run organization at the University of California, Berkeley, dedicated to serving the cryptocurrency and blockchain communities at the university and greater East Bay region. It hosts a range of events and programs to promote blockchain and offers open-source undergraduate cryptocurrency courses.

Blockchain Council
340 S. Lemon Ave. #1147
Walnut, CA 91789
phone: (323) 984-8594
email: hello@blockchain-council.org
website: www.blockchain-council.org

The Blockchain Council is a private organization of blockchain subject experts and enthusiasts that runs a variety of training sessions, webinars, and workshops on the use of blockchain. The Blockchain Council also offers non-accredited certifications and degrees in both Blockchain use and cryptocurrency trading.

Blockchain Education Network (BEN)
email: contact@blockchainedu.org
website: blockchainedu.org

The Blockchain Education Network is an international student organization that partners with education organizations around the world to educate and empower students who are interested in blockchain technology. BEN is largely made up of students and college alumni who create bitcoin and blockchain clubs on academic campuses.

Codementor: Blockchain Learning Center
email: support@codementor.io
website: www.codementor.io/learn/blockchain

Codementor is an open marketplace platform for experienced web developers to offer live help, long-term mentorship, and team training courses on the programming languages or web technology they specialize in, with rates set by the mentor themselves. The organization's Blockchain Learning Center contains a collection of curated resources to help students learn blockchain programming and keep up-to-date with the latest developments in blockchain technology.

Cryptocurrency Academy
Shrosha Street 2, Office 7a
Tbilisi, Georgia
phone: +31 6 11 36 27 77
email: info@cryptocurrency.nu
website: www.cryptocurrency.nu

The Cryptocurrency Academy is a group managed by Silicon Valley professionals that shares links to interesting ICOs (initial coin offerings), livestreams various conferences that members attend, and highlights compelling articles on cryptocurrency.

Federal Reserve Bank of St. Louis
Federal Reserve Bank Plaza
1 Broadway
St. Louis, MO 63102
phone: (314) 444-8444
email: research@stlouisfed.org
webstie: www.stlouisfed.org

The Federal Reserve Bank of St. Louis is one of the twelve Federal Reserve banks in the country and has done extensive research into the possibility of utilizing cryptocurrencies. Their research department's website offers reports and studies on the history and development of blockchain technology and explains some of the reservations that a central bank like the Federal Reserve would have about currencies that use blockchain technology.

Global Blockchain Business Council
1440 G St. NW (9th floor)
Washington, DC 20005
email: info@gbbcouncil.org
website: www.gbbcouncil.org

The Global Blockchain Business Council is the leading trade association for the blockchain technology ecosystem, which formally launched during the 2017 Annual World Economic Forum in Davos, Switzerland.

The Government Blockchain Association

website: www.gbaglobal.org

The Government Blockchain Association is a US-based nonprofit organization that consists of individuals and organizations that are interested in promoting blockchain-related solutions to government problems.

North America Blockchain Association

1601 McCarthy Blvd

Milpitas, CA 95035

email: info@nablockchain.org

website: nablockchain.org

The North America Blockchain Association is a nonprofit organization that aims to initiate, connect, organize, and facilitate blockchain technology initiatives. Recently, the organization has begun working with RealChain, a group that attempts to pair high-end luxury goods with customers on the blockchain.

The World Blockchain Organization

email: info@unwbo.org

website: www.unwbo.org

The World Blockchain Organization is an NGO registered with the United Nations Department of Economic and Social Affairs. It promotes blockchain technology as a driver of economic growth, inclusive development, and environmental sustainability, and offers leadership and support in advancing knowledge and blockchain policies worldwide.

Bibliography

Books

Saifedean Ammous. *The Bitcoin Standard: The Decentralized Alternative to Central Banking.* Hoboken, NJ: Wiley, 2018.

Andreas M. Antonopoulos. *The Internet of Money.* Columbia, MD: Merkle Bloom, 2016.

Dean Armstrong, Dan Hyde, and Sam Thomas. *Blockchain and Cryptocurrency: Legal and Regulatory Challenges.* London: Bloomsbury, 2019.

Nick Bilton. *American Kingpin: The Epic Hunt for the Criminal Mastermind Behind the Silk Road.* New York, NY: Portfolio, 2017.

Phil Champagne, ed. *The Book Of Satoshi: The Collected Writings of Bitcoin Creator Satoshi Nakamoto.* Seattle, WA: Amazon Digital Services, 2014.

George Gilder. *Life After Google: The Fall of Big Data and the Rise of the Blockchain Economy.* Washington, DC: Gateway Editions, 2018.

John Hargrave. *Blockchain for Everyone: Unlock the Secrets of the New Millionaire Class.* New York, NY: Simon & Schuster, 2019.

Frederic Laloux and Ken Wilber. *Reinventing Organizations.* Millis, MA: Nelson Parker, 2014.

Andrew McAfee and Erik Brynjolfsson. *Machine, Platform, Crowd: Harnessing Our Digital Future.* New York, NY: W.W. Norton & Company, 2018.

Marcus O'Dair. *Distributed Creativity: How Blockchain Technology Will Transform the Creative Economy.* London, UK: Palgrave Macmillan, 2019.

Nathaniel Popper. *Digital Gold: Bitcoin and the Inside Story of the Misfits and Millionaires Trying to Reinvent Money*. New York, NY: Harper, 2015.

Don Tapscott and Alex Tapscott. *Blockchain Revolution: How the Technology Behind Bitcoin Is Changing Money, Business, and the World*. New York, NY: Portfolio, 2016.

Paul Vigna and Michael J. Casey. *The Age of Cryptocurrency: How Bitcoin and Digital Money Are Challenging the Global Economic Order*. New York, NY: Macmillan, 2015.

Paul Vigna and Michael J. Casey. *The Truth Machine: The Blockchain and the Future of Everything*. New York, NY: St. Martins, 2018.

Stephen P. Williams. *Blockchain: The Next Everything*. New York, NY: Simon & Schuster, 2019.

Periodicals and Internet Sources

Joshua Davis, "The Crypto-Currency," *New Yorker*, October 10, 2018. www.newyorker.com/magazine/2011/10/10/the-crypto-currency.

Paul Ford, "Bitcoin Is Ridiculous. Blockchain Is Dangerous," *Bloomberg*, March 9, 2018. www.bloomberg.com/news/features/2018-03-09/bitcoin-is-ridiculous-blockchain-is-dangerous-paul-ford.

Steven Johnson, "Beyond the Bitcoin Bubble," *New York Times Magazine*, January 16, 2018. www.nytimes.com/2018/01/16/magazine/beyond-the-bitcoin-bubble.html.

Gideon Lewis-Kraus, "Inside the Crypto World's Biggest Scandal," *Wired*, June 19, 2018. www.wired.com/story/tezos-blockchain-love-story-horror-story.

Christopher Mims, "Why Blockchain Will Survive, Even If Bitcoin Doesn't," *Wall Street Journal*, March 11, 2018. www.wsj.com/articles/why-blockchain-will-survive-even-if-bitcoin-doesnt-1520769600.

Glen Mpufane and Brian Kohler, "The Lure of the Quick Technological Fix: Blockchain and the Case of Cobalt," *International Union Rights*, 2018, Vol. 25, No. 3.

Mike Orcutt, "In 2019, Blockchains Will Start to Become Boring," *MIT Technology Review*, January 2, 2019. www.technologyreview.com/s/612687/in-2019-blockchains-will-start-to-become-boring.

Nick Paumgarten, "The Prophets of Cryptocurrency Survey the Boom and Bust," *New Yorker*, October 22, 2018. www.newyorker.com/magazine/2018/10/22/the-prophets-of-cryptocurrency-survey-the-boom-and-bust.

Marc Pilkington, "Can Global Elites Pave the Way for a New Transnational Unit of Account? A Reflection on the Numerical Nature of Money," *World Review of Political Economy*, Winter 2015.

Gary Shteyngart, "A Sidelined Wall Street Legend Bets on Bitcoin," *New Yorker*, April 16, 2018. www.newyorker.com/magazine/2018/04/16/a-sidelined-wall-street-legend-bets-on-bitcoin.

Andrew Ross Sorkin, "Demystifying the Blockchain," *New York Times*, June 27, 2018. www.nytimes.com/2018/06/27/business/dealbook/blockchain-technology.html.

Misha Tsukerman, "The Block Is Hot: A Survey of the State of Bitcoin Regulation and Suggestions for the Future," *Berkeley Technology Law Journal*, 2015, Vol. 30, No. 4.

Tunku Varadarajan, "The Blockchain Is the Internet of Money," *Wall Street Journal*, Sept. 22, 2017. www.wsj.com/articles/the-blockchain-is-the-internet-of-money-1506119424.

Index

A

Africa, 134–136, 138–147
Andreessen, Marc, 30
anti-money laundering (AML),
    69, 95–98, 104, 106,
    116–117

B

bank deposits, 61–67
bitcoin, 30, 31, 32, 33, 37–40,
    74, 78, 90, 110, 111,
    115–117, 120–121
    hard fork, 56, 58, 74, 87, 108,
        112, 121, 135
    regulation of, 102–108,
        109–114, 115–119
    taxation, 102, 106, 107
bitcoin bubble, 78–80, 125, 160
bitcoin exchange, 49, 88, 96,
    106, 116, 121, 141–143
BitLicense, 115, 117–119, 159
blockchain, 19–24, 28, 30–33,
    34–36, 37–40, 90, 99, 110,
    111–112, 123, 139–140
    alternative blockchain, 33
    as electronic ledger, 153–160
    sidechain, 33, 57
    voting technology, 161–165
Buffet, Warren, 51–52

C

cash, 37, 60, 62–63, 64–65, 110,
    116, 136, 145
CBDC (central bank-issued
    digital currency), 80–84
central banks, 27–29, 42–43,
    52 60–67, 68–70, 77–78,
    81–84, 92, 95, 105, 109,
    114,
China, 75, 85–90, 106, 112, 114
Codius, 32
colored coins, 33, 68
cryptocurrency, 14, 19–21, 25–
    26, 28–29, 32–36, 41–47,
    55, 68–70, 72, 77–78, 84,
    92–94, 95–98, 102–114,
    120–122, 138, 147
    decentralization, 21, 85,
        102, 110, 111, 120–123,
        154–155
    as financial investment, 47,
        49–52
    payment method, 48, 51,
        60–70, 77, 80, 89, 93,
        116, 122, 134
    regulation of, 23, 88, 102–108,
        109–114, 115–119, 103–
        108, 134–135, 145–146
    as speculative investment,
        41–42, 44, 50–52, 89,
        125, 159

volatility, 22, 35, 43–45, 49, 52, 65, 78, 88, 103–109, 152

Cryptokitty, 57, 124

currency, 14–16, 25–26, 30–34, 39–40, 41–46, 47–51, 60–71, 74–76
  digital, 47, 60–71, 77, 81, 82
  gold standard, 26, 39, 44, 60–61, 72–74
  medium of exchange, 39, 41, 44–46, 48, 63, 87
  scarcity, verifiability, and availability, 24–25, 27, 28–29
  virtual, 47, 61–62, 63–69, 77, 89, 105, 113, 129, 140

D

Dark Web, 102–103

digital wallet, 20, 36, 47, 49, 78, 82–83, 92– 93, 96–97, 105, 110, 138–139

Dimon, Jamie, 51–52, 79, 109

distributed ledger technology (DLT), 133–137

Dogecoin, 120, 121

E

environmental hazards, 148–151

Equifax data breach, 23

Ethereum, 19, 32, 36, 39, 57, 95, 109, 120, 124, 139, 160

euro, 42, 45, 63

European Union, 105, 141

F

Fedcoin, 68–69, 114

Federal Deposit Insurance Corporation, 49

fiat currency, 22, 26–28, 36, 41–42, 45, 47, 68, 82, 96–98, 142, 145, 158

G

Greenspan, Alan, 25, 51

H

hackers, 23, 49, 95, 111–112, 114, 162, 164

hash function, 19–21

Hodl, 72, 78

Hyperledger, 21, 58

I

information asymmetries, 127–132

initial coin offering (ICO), 110, 113, 138, 159

K

know your client (KYC), 69, 96–98, 104, 106, 116–117

L

liquidity, 42–43, 49–50, 63, 66, 84, 135
Litecoin, 45, 46, 56, 120, 121, 139

M

miners, 15, 33–38, 44, 62, 72–74, 78, 97–98, 101, 111–112, 121, 123–124, 148–150
mining, 21, 29, 33, 36, 62, 72–75, 86–87, 90, 94, 104, 111–112, 124, 148–150
Monero, 45, 57
money laundering, 46, 64, 88, 95–98, 102–103, 105, 134
Mt. Gox, 49

N

Nakamoto, Satoshi, 72, 79, 111, 139
Namecoin, 56
next generation, 55, 57–59

P

private key, 20, 28, 74
proof-of-stake (PoS), 23, 58
proof-of-work (PoW), 21, 56, 58, 73, 86, 100, 101
public key cryptography, 20–21, 28, 59, 164

S

Sawtooth, 58
Shiller, Robert, 51
Silk Road marketplace, 102
smart contracts, 31, 32, 35–36, 57, 81, 123, 129–132, 154, 158–160
supply and demand, 51–53
Swiss National Bank, 61, 64, 81
Szabo, Nick, 32

U

United States, 26, 46, 47, 103–104
US Commodity Futures Trading Commission (CFTC), 104
US Federal Reserve, 22, 27, 42, 43, 47
US Mint, 47
US Securities and Exchange Commission (SEC), 104
US Treasury, 47, 104

W

Wikipedia, 99–101

Z

Zcash, 45, 56, 57